To:

_____

From:

_____

Celebrating
Every Kind *of* Mom

Published by B&H Publishing Group
Nashville, Tennessee

Dewey Decimal Classification: 248.843

Subject Heading: MOTHERS / WOMEN / DAUGHTERS

Cover design and lettering by Emily Strnad.
Additional design by Katherin Hamm.

1 2 3 4 5 6 7 • 24 23 22 21 20

Celebrating
Every Kind *of* Mom

by (in)courage
Anna Rendell, General Editor

PUBLISHING
NASHVILLE, TENNESSEE

Contents

Introduction

We are the moms who hug, dance, and snuggle. We are the moms who get overwhelmed, whose snarls sometimes come easier than our smiles. We are the moms who live in the push-pull of exhaustion and joy, in the tumultuous world of feelings and guilt and giving all of ourselves.

We are the moms who pray our children will fly while a tiny part of our heart grieves their flight from us, because we are the moms who love those children with every fiber of our being. We're not sure where they end and we begin, but we know we didn't begin until they arrived.

We are the moms who work around the clock in a million different ways. Praying. Cooking. Cleaning up. Carpooling to school and dropping off at daycare. Guiding. Loving, always loving. Scolding and worrying. Kissing boo-boos and wiping tears. Breathing deep, in and out, over and over. Chasing their feet and their hearts. Answering emails in the middle of the night. Pulling them back and drawing them in and sending them out. Scrubbing toilets and remembering details and packing lunches and signing papers and pouring out.

We are the moms who love children we didn't birth. We are the neighbors, aunties, sisters, friends, and church grandmas who love these kids as though they're our own. We snuggle up during the sermon at church to beloved little ones and pass them hard candies to squelch the wiggles. We attend birthday parties and graduations and weddings, bearing gifts for these dear hearts, setting up tables and making food and then cleaning up at the end of the day. We rock little babies and help big kids pack for college, tearing up at the thought of them driving away. We light up when our phone dings and it's a text from that precious high schooler. We read stories and sing songs and carefully choose cards to pop in the mail for every holiday.

We are the moms who haven't had a night out in ages, and who crave one like oxygen. Who run on grace and caffeine. Who build a meal off of the scraps pilfered from kids' plates. Who go through more coffee shop drive-throughs than we care to admit. Who are exhausted from being "on" all day at work, and coming home to be "on" all night.

We are the moms who drive through McDonald's for milk because we're out at home and just cannot drag ourselves into the actual grocery store. Who pay for a latte in change dug out from between the minivan seats. Who cannot make it to church without bickering with our family on the drive. Who are consistently seven minutes late to every appointment. Who perpetually lose socks to the washing machine, and have been known to purchase new underwear instead of washing the pairs we already own. Who take our alone time seriously and guard it fiercely—just like we do our kids.

We are the moms who long for more. More grace. More patience. More coffee. More time (always more time). More space—in home and heart. More money. More sleep. More Christ in us. More life in our days. More quiet.

At the same time, we are the moms who long for less. Less laundry. Less fighting. Less yelling. Less clutter. Less selfishness. Less guilt. Less busy. Less stuff. Less dust. Less hustle.

We are the moms who sit in the hallway in tears during bedtime, drained. The moms who sit in empty houses in tears because there are no more babies to tuck in at bedtime. We are the moms who ache for those we've lost, for those we've wanted, for those we've asked for, for those whom we've begged God about and bruised our knees in earnest prayer. For the babies we couldn't carry. For the children we've lost to heaven and red tape. For the grown children we couldn't hold on to as they flew our coop to make their lives. For waywards and prodigals and could've-beens.

We love this life even when we don't like it very much. We love these kids with all of our being—even when we may not like them very much.

We thank God for the gift of love He gives in the form of sticky hands, flown coops, late nights, early mornings, birthday celebrations, cards in the mail, trips to see each other, texts sent, calls placed, and prayers whispered.

We are these moms, and this book is for us all.

May you find yourself and someone you love amidst these pages. May you be inspired, uplifted, refreshed, and renewed to go forth and love those kids. This is for you, one-of-a-kind mom!

#
That Breaks the Mold

One of the most important women in my life isn't related to me at all, yet my kids call her Grandma. She loves our family and has taken us all under her heart as if her own. She is a woman whose love has broken the mold of what is often considered family.

Countless women don't hold children in their arms or raise them in their homes. They are affectionately known as bonus moms, church grandmas, aunties, nanas, and a number of other titles. These women celebrate birthdays, cook meals, give rides, help with laundry, and offer love to their "extra" kids, grandkids, nieces, nephews, neighbors, and kids at church, and their presence in our lives is imperative. What would our village be without them? Pretty empty, that's what.

This section is full of stories for and about these mothers, the precious women who break the mold of motherhood. These are women throughout Scripture—and in our lives—who gave of themselves when it wasn't a requirement or demand, but simply out of an abundance of love.

To the "bonus moms" of the world . . . thank you. Bless you. You are adored and needed and loved beyond measure.

Mothering Is . . .

Mothering may not look like what we thought it would look like.

It doesn't look like it does in the movies or TV shows. Or most of our social media feeds. Or our friends' lives. Or any version of what we thought it would look like at all.

It may look like loving other people's children. It may look like loving your neighbors, your nephews and nieces, the kids growing up in your home, and the kids growing up in your church.

Mothering looks like life lived between. The shots between frames shared online. The moments that go unnoticed, the tiny spaces between the highs and lows. Right there, between the funny and the serious.

Mothering looks like sharing our food with sticky little fingers and insatiable teenagers. In the minds of my children, anything sitting on my plate, going to be on my plate, used to be on my plate, in my hand, in my mouth, next to me, or that I am considering eating is fair game. The same applies to beverages. Mothering is grocery shopping—again. Keeping a stocked pantry for the high schoolers who plow through before starting homework on your kitchen table. It's pulling in a drive-thru for burgers. It's making sure to tuck treats into your purse before church for the littles who will inch up next to you during the sermon. It's baking their favorite cookies and bringing them next door, their mom smiling with relief at the welcome sight of you (and the full cookie tin). It's testing a new recipe for a beloved nephew's birthday cake only to realize that the recipe is not a winner, and then running to the grocery store for a backup cake just before the family arrives at your home for dessert.

It's applying sunscreen to every inch of our kids' exposed skin while forgetting to apply it to ourselves.

It's walking slowly next to a toddler who "can do it herself!"

It's coaching a middle schooler through feeling *all the feelings* they have in a day while somehow simultaneously finishing a school project the night before it's due.

Mothering is saying, "I'm heading up to bed" and not actually crawling in for another half hour, because of all the stops along the way to pick up each abandoned toy, put dishes in the sink, sweep up stray crumbs, fill the dog's water bowl, peek in on the sleeping kids, wash our face, quickly scroll on our phone, peek on the kids again, and then finally turn out the light until we turn it back on again when a kid wakes up. There's a season for good sleep; often, mothering is not that season.

> *For everything there is a season,*
> *a time for every activity under heaven.*
> ECCLESIASTES 3:1 (NLT)

Mothering is rarely being alone. It's soaking up each and every last second of alone time (even at work or the dentist), because it is precious. It's pushing away guilt for loving that alone time so much. It's fighting the urge to check in with the family every ten minutes while you're away.

It's carrying the baby all morning, putting her down so you can use the bathroom, and picking her right back up when she cries.

Mothering is quietly completing the tasks no one will see but everyone would miss if left undone. Birthday cards and phone calls to family. Calendar keeping. Household maintaining. Replacing toothbrushes.

Cleaning toilets. Returning library books. The tasks that never cease. The tasks that keep to-do lists in business. The tasks that pop into our minds, getting us out of bed in the middle of the night to quickly complete them before they flee our minds.

It's braces and marching band and new sneakers. It's driving into rush hour traffic to make it to the birthday dinner on time. It's sending Valentine cards and wrapping Christmas gifts and remembering each precious heart in prayer.

Mothering is snuggles early in the morning. It's hair-smoothing late at night. It's making choices that are hard, but right for you and your kids. It's letting your kids go. It's holding your kids close. It's tender moments that make you teary with their sweetness, and flushed with anger, and overcome with gratitude—all in the span of a single day.

Mothering is offering a prayer when you have no words to utter.

In the same way, the Spirit helps us in our weakness.
We do not know what we ought to pray for,
but the Spirit himself intercedes for us through wordless groans.

ROMANS 8:26 (NIV)

Mothering is delightful, difficult, beautiful, brutal, blessed, terrifying, sweet, good, and hard.

Mothering is surprising, mundane, ordinary, and extraordinary.

Mothering is tender, fierce, glorious, gritty, and a gift.

Mothering may not look a thing like you thought it would. It may not be anything like you pictured. But no matter what it looks like to you, for you, mothering is everything.

Give all your worries to God,

for he cares about you.

I PETER 5:7 (NLT)

For Motherless Daughters

I grew up with my maternal grandmother. I never lived solely with my mother; she had tremendous issues and struggles that made it impossible for her to take care of a child.

Although my grandmother raised me, practically since birth, I never viewed her as my mother. I always knew that my mother existed, but for whatever reason, decided not to raise me. As you can imagine, this will mess with a child's mind. I have been plagued with all manner of insecurities, unyielding feelings of unworthiness, and feelings of being unlovable. I often wondered if there was something wrong with me.

I spent most of my childhood with an unconscious desire to be mothered by my mother, but it never happened. She drifted in and out of my life like the ocean's tides. Eventually, that became okay with me. She had her life and I had mine, and as time went by, our two lives rarely intersected.

As sad as all of this appears, this was my life. This is what I had always known.

But with the distance that time brings, as I reflect on my childhood, I can see clearly that the fingerprints of God were all over it! That lack of mothering actually drove me to seek out older women who would love and encourage me. Even before I knew Christ, during my junior high and high school years, God placed a couple of amazing teachers in my life who took time and invested in me.

Through the past twenty years of my following Jesus, He has been more than faithful to overflow my life with spiritual mothers. These women, these mothers have . . .

Loved me,

Encouraged me,

Blessed me,

Corrected me,

Taught me,

Wept with me,

Rejoiced with me,

Served me,

Prayed with me, and

Prayed for me.

Each and every one of them has in some way helped to shape my walk with the Lord. Scripture tells us that older women should instruct younger women in the ways of God. And now, in my late thirties and single, without biological kids of my own, I have the privilege of being a spiritual mom myself to some precious junior high and high school girls at my church. It is one of the deepest joys of my life.

As women, we are called to both mother and to be mothered. This happens no matter how old you are or what season of life you are in. This call from the Lord transcends biology, and even expectation. Whether you too know the pain that comes from being a motherless daughter, the ache that emerges from wishing for children to fill your home, or the joy that flows from being a spiritual mom, know that you are deeply loved by a God who is faithful to fill our empty spaces.

Love That Breaks the Mold

Jochebed and Pharaoh's Daughter

Now a man from the family of Levi married a Levite woman. The woman became pregnant and gave birth to a son; when she saw that he was beautiful, she hid him for three months. But when she could no longer hide him, she got a papyrus basket for him and coated it with asphalt and pitch. She placed the child in it and set it among the reeds by the bank of the Nile. Then his sister stood at a distance in order to see what would happen to him.

Pharaoh's daughter went down to bathe at the Nile while her servant girls walked along the riverbank. She saw the basket among the reeds, sent her slave girl, took it, opened it, and saw him, the child—and there he was, a little boy, crying. She felt sorry for him and said, "This is one of the Hebrew boys."

Then his sister said to Pharaoh's daughter, "Should I go and call a Hebrew woman who is nursing to nurse the boy for you?"

"Go," Pharaoh's daughter told her. So the girl went and called the boy's mother. Then Pharaoh's daughter said to her, "Take this child and nurse him for me, and I will pay your wages." So the woman took the boy and nursed him. When the child grew older, she brought him to Pharaoh's daughter, and he became her son. She named him Moses, "Because," she said, "I drew him out of the water."

EXODUS 2:1–10

Jochebed, Moses' mother, was a woman of great bravery. Her worst nightmare had come true. Her baby boy's life was in danger, and she could no longer hide him. So, she enacted a plan to save her son's life. With no idea if it world work, Jochebed placed her son, Moses, in a basket in the river, and God rewarded her bravery. He allowed Pharaoh's daughter to find the basket with baby Moses inside, who then asked Jochebed to care for him until he was old enough to live in the palace.

If this mother had let fear control her actions, she would have missed out on a miracle. Because Jochebed chose to be brave, she got to watch God care for Moses and Jochebed's entire family, protecting them and bringing about His purposes.

Jochebed's obedience and bravery also created a whole new family, allowing Pharaoh's daughter to become an adoptive mother. Pharaoh's daughter showed great bravery as well, as she boldly defied her father's orders to kill all infant boys. Instead, she took Moses in as her own.

All families—even the ones in the Bible—are messy, and each mother has a unique story regarding how her children came to be hers. Jochebed, Moses, and Pharaoh's daughter are no exception; rather, they're an example of grace, bravery, and love that breaks the mold.

A Different Kind of Brave

The day I delivered our first baby girl was filled with joy and grief for my husband and me. We were in complete bliss as I picked out which outfit she would wear for her pictures with her big brother. As the nurses wheeled her out, I remember turning the television on to pass the time until my baby was back in my arms. The words "BREAKING NEWS" caught my attention.

A shooting had taken place in an elementary school, and the station was broadcasting live footage of parents waiting for news of their children. It suddenly felt like all the air had been sucked out of the room. There I was in a hospital bed waiting for the life I brought into this world, as these parents waited for the worst.

I remember crying for those parents and those innocent children. When my baby was placed in my arms, I held her a little tighter. The headlines can sometimes shake us to the core of our souls, and fear can consume us if we let it. I think of Moses' mother, Jochebed, and how scared she must have been when she learned that her baby was a boy. She lived in a corrupt time when all baby boys were thrown into the river.

And yet, instead of letting fear control her, she kept her son with love in her heart and strength in her soul. When she could no longer hide him, she did the hardest thing she'd ever have to do. She coated a basket with asphalt and pitch and placed her baby boy in it. Then she placed him in the reeds among the Nile.

When I used to think of the word *brave*, I imagined someone fighting off lions and bears. But it also looks a lot like a mother trusting in God and gently placing her child into the waters of the unknown. The most beautiful part of the story is that God is faithful in all He does, and He returned Moses to Jochebed for a season, before Moses made his way to the palace under the care of Pharaoh's daughter.

Since the birth of my first daughter and the day of that horrendous news, we've welcomed three more children into this world. As parents in this day and age, we may not be called to release our children into the river in baskets, but we are called to release them to God. Each time we do, we find that His provision is always better than we could ever imagine.

Fear still creeps in some days, especially since I will soon have little ones in public school. But in spite of fearing the unknown waters, I want to love relentlessly, fervently trusting in God with faith like Jochebed. I want to live a life of faith, and most of all, I want to live life with a different kind of brave.

Reflections

How can you bravely show your love for the children God has trusted you with?

_____

_____

_____

_____

_____

_____

_____

_____

_____

_____

_____

_____

_____

_____

_____

_____

"For the Lᴏʀᴅ your God is living among you.

He is a mighty savior.

He will take delight in you with gladness.

With his love, he will calm all your fears.

He will rejoice over you with joyful songs."

ZEPHANIAH 3:17 (NLT)

Tiny Acts of Service, Big Celebration

Over the past week I have planned and cooked meals, scrubbed toilets, purchased white string cheese for one child and orange string cheese for another, ordered more tissues and dish soap to arrive on my doorstep, and vacuumed up dog hair under the table.

I've filled out the school permission slips and book orders that I found in backpacks. I've changed my kids' closets over for both size and seasons; today I'm diving into the shoes to do the same. I've sent pictures to be developed for "Star of the Week" day at preschool, then packed the photos up in a labeled envelope and put it alongside the requested favorite book in a backpack.

I've restocked the shower with body wash and distributed toilet paper to all the various empty rolls. I've wiped counters and cleared the table in one fell swoop. I've prayed with and for my kids and tucked little curls behind little ears at night—both ears, not just one, because I know she likes it tucked behind both.

I've brushed and wiggled teeth and hollered for hands to be washed (I don't need to see them to know they're dirty). I've helped with math homework and texted pictures to Grandma. I've tossed favorite T-shirts into the washing machine and poured water in the dog's bowl. I've watered the preschool plant project and moved it into the sunshine to try and keep it alive another day.

All in a week. A very typical, run-of-the-mill week. Extraordinary all mixed up with the mundane.

As a mother and woman, I constantly perform acts of tiny service that go unseen. All day, every day. The bittiest of details, done with barely a thought. Just thirty-seven years into being a woman and eight years into mothering, I'm still learning these are finely tuned, carefully honed skills and marks of the craft.

And because you are a woman and a mother in your own unique way, I know you likely do the same.

We are the managers of the minutiae, keepers of the details that make a home run and hearts sing, whether that home is a small apartment with roommates or farm house with kids and chickens running wild. We are the knowers of small things, of favorites and things not-so-loved. We can read a heart in one glance. We can heal with a hug. We can calm with a word. We are the hosts of each other, the middle-of-the-night texters, the hearts that reach out when we feel a friend needs us.

Moms, caretakers, grandmas, babysitters, teachers . . . every one of us is a mother of sorts, and as such, we are the unseen do-ers. We are the people of hidden service, who have learned to do things swiftly and silently in a second-nature sort of way. At times, that has rendered me feeling powerless and small. Unimportant and unimpressive. Even though I know that if I disappeared, tasks would be left undone (Hello, favorite T-shirt going unwashed. Hi, dog hair unvacuumed for a week.) and all the things I set in place could fall apart, it's easy to throw an "I don't matter" pity party for myself. It's easy for me to look to my husband, kids, coworkers, roommates, or friends for affirmation that may never come.

It's a good thing we have a God who adores and affirms women.

We have a God who appeared first to women after rising, who believes in women and has used their hands throughout history to do His good work, who sees us—both as we are and as we will be.

We have a God who sees motherhood as a valuable calling, and in His wisdom gifts us individually to mother others in the place we are.

Each and every one of those invisible tasks is seen, etched in His mind as He delights in you.

> "For the LORD your God is living among you.
>   He is a mighty savior.
> He will take delight in you with gladness.
>   With his love, he will calm all your fears.
> He will rejoice over you with joyful songs."
> ZEPHANIAH 3:17 (NLT)

He. Delights. In. You.

Yep, you. You, who are a weary mother. You, who are not a mom to children of your blood. You, in the office cubicle. You, who diligently serves on the behind-the-scenes committees at church. You, who texts your friends to check in. You, who hasn't had an evening to herself in way, way too long. You, who loves being a mom. You, the woman who maintains countless unseen tasks, holds things together (sometimes by a thread), and balances plates like a boss.

You are beloved by Him. God delights in His daughters. The end.

When I was a kid, my own mom used to tell us, "I am woman. Hear me roar!" as she tarred the driveway, hung sheetrock in the basement, juggled our schedules and her jobs, and tenderly cared for her parents, her family, and her friends.

May we roar. May we celebrate our sisters and friends as they find their own roars. And may we feel the glow of love from our God who adores us, and who sees every tiny act of service.

A Love That Breaks the Mold

Ruth and Naomi

During the time of the judges, there was a famine in the land. A man left Bethlehem in Judah with his wife and two sons to stay in the territory of Moab for a while. The man's name was Elimelech, and his wife's name was Naomi. The names of his two sons were Mahlon and Chilion. They were Ephrathites from Bethlehem in Judah. They entered the fields of Moab and settled there. Naomi's husband Elimelech died, and she was left with her two sons. Her sons took Moabite women as their wives: one was named Orpah and the second was named Ruth. After they lived in Moab about ten years, both Mahlon and Chilion also died, and Naomi was left without her two children and without her husband.

She and her daughters-in-law set out to return from the territory of Moab, because she had heard in Moab that the Lord had paid attention to his people's need by providing them food. She left the place where she had been living, accompanied by her two daughters-in-law, and traveled along the road leading back to the land of Judah.

RUTH 1:1–7

A severe famine led Naomi's family to the neighboring country of Moab, but after Naomi's husband and two sons died at an early age, she was left alone in a foreign land. Without any way to provide for herself, she returned to Israel a broken, bitter woman. Convinced God had turned His back on her, Naomi didn't believe the Lord would change her situation, but the faithfulness of her daughter-in-law Ruth began to change her heart.

Because Ruth stayed.

She could have left Naomi, her widowed mother-in-law, to fend for herself as she traveled back to her native home in Israel. Ruth, a widow herself, could have gone back to her own people in the land of Moab. But she stayed. Even after Naomi had lost all hope, Ruth chose to remain by Naomi's side and provide for them by gleaning whatever the harvesters left behind in the fields. Ruth was a faithful daughter-in-law, and even more so, a faithful friend.

Through Ruth's friendship, God slowly softened Naomi's heart. With Ruth by her side, Naomi could see the Lord's provision in their lives. In His timing God redeemed her story, allowing her to hold and care for a new grandson. Despite the years of brokenness, Naomi lived to see the beauty that came from her suffering. And ultimately, God blessed their unconventional family with a son and grandson, continuing to use them as a family who broke the mold.

When Nothing Is Left but Love

I was in my early thirties, established in my career, and comfortable in my skin, but I was still nervous when the time came to meet my future mother-in-law. Would she like me as a person, approve of me as a daughter-in-law, accept me into the family, even with my bad-girl past?

Our first meeting was cordial, and she always made me welcome in her home. But as each year went by, I became less certain of my place in her heart and held her at arm's length emotionally. Yes, I dutifully sent flowers each Mother's Day, made her favorite dish for Thanksgiving, and showered her with presents at Christmas. But whether it was pride, anxiety, or insecurity, something kept me from building a nest for her in my heart.

Then I studied the book of Ruth. Undone by the loving-kindness Ruth showed her mother-in-law, Naomi, I realized something had to change in my life—and that something was me.

A phone call to my mother-in-law seemed the place to begin. My hand shook as I punched in the numbers. I had no real plan, trusting God to give me the words to say: *I'm sorry. Please forgive me. I love you. Can we begin again?*

When my mother-in-law answered the phone, an overwhelming sense of peace washed over me. Whatever fears I'd harbored—of rejection, of losing her as I'd lost my own mother, of not measuring up—were gone. Nothing was left but love.

The next time we visited my in-law's house, I wrapped my arms around her and gave her my first real hug. Our last five years together were sweeter than all the years that came before then, combined. I have Ruth the Moabitess to thank for that, and the Lord she vowed to follow.

When Naomi started for home after ten years in the far country of Moab, she urged her two daughters-in-law, Orpah and Ruth, to return to Moab and to their gods. Orpah was convinced; Ruth was not. She told Naomi, *"Don't plead with me to abandon you or to return and not follow you. For wherever you go, I will go, and wherever you live, I will live; your people will be my people, and your God will be my God"* (Ruth 1:16).

Ruth was determined not to go back to her false gods. We can't say for sure, but sometimes I wonder if the Spirit of God moved through Ruth like living water in that moment—cleansing her, filling her, making her altogether new. One thing we can know is that Ruth wasn't merely making a choice to follow her mother-in-law. Her decision included a commitment to the Lord Himself, the God of the Israelites.

God alone ordained and orchestrated this sacred moment. Ruth's great-grandson would one day write, *"The counsel of the LORD stands forever, the plans of his heart from generation to generation"* (Ps. 33:11). Naomi and Ruth are woven into those plans. So are you, beloved. Long before Naomi and Ruth walked the earth, God's plans for you were already in place.

Before Naomi could respond that day, Ruth made a bold vow: *"For wherever you go, I will go"* (Ruth 1:16). More than one dewy-eyed bride has repeated Ruth's words while gazing into her bridegroom's handsome face. But Ruth wasn't talking to or about a man. She was speaking to and about her mother-in-law, who by all appearances didn't want her daughter-in-law along for the ride.

Ruth's second vow is equally powerful: *"and wherever you live, I will live"* (v. 16). She'd never been to Bethlehem, yet seemed to care little about where she was going, as long as she was with Naomi. She continued, *"your people will be my people"* (v. 16). It's one thing to leave your house and quite another to leave your country. Ruth promised to adopt the laws, traditions, dialect, foods, customs, folklore, and history of Israel, turning her back on the only life she knew and embracing a world she had yet to experience.

We've seen Ruth's courage and commitment on display. Next comes her extraordinary leap of faith: *"and your God will be my God"* (v. 16). Over the years, Naomi had plenty of time to teach her daughter-in-law about the covenant with Abraham and the exodus with Moses. She'd also had countless Sabbaths to show Ruth what a life devoted to the one true God looked like. Yet in the end, it was God at work in Ruth's heart that made her confession of faith possible.

If you have a mother-in-law, Ruth's brave example shows how you can strengthen or rebuild your one-of-a-kind relationship. Perhaps some of these practical ideas might help:

- Praise her good points. Just as you may wonder if your mother-in-law likes you, she may think you don't like her. So, praise her every chance you get and help put her unspoken fears to rest.

- Brag about her son. At any age, mothers long to know they did a good job. Sincerely compliment your husband's fine character or commendable actions, then watch his mother light up.

- Request a favorite recipe. Gourmet or otherwise, her home-cooked meals fed your growing husband. Find out his favorite dish and ask his mother to share the recipe.

- Give thanks. Show your gratitude for the woman who raised the man you love. She wasn't a perfect mother, but she was his mother. She still is, and always will be.

As relationships go, this one can be complicated, which means it also has the potential to go deep and wide. Open your heart, friend. Let her in.

Reflections

How can you honor your mother-in-law, or another older mother figure in your life?

_____

_____

_____

_____

_____

_____

_____

_____

_____

_____

_____

_____

_____

_____

_____

_____

First a Friend, Then a Family

I grew up with two younger siblings and a single mom. My dad filed for divorce when my siblings and I were the same age as my kids are right now—seven, five, and three.

My mom was a superhero.

She worked two jobs: one as a fifth-grade band director at an elementary school and another as the choir director at our church. Between working days, evenings, and weekends, chauffeuring my siblings and I all over creation to our many extracurricular activities, and doing the double share of daily tasks like cooking, cleaning, shopping, bedtime, homework help, and the like, her life didn't leave a lot of spare time for friendships. But she did the best she could with what she had, as we all do, and she made time for friends.

My mom didn't attend any "girls' nights out," and she never met friends for coffee, but I did see her talk on the telephone. The long, blue, spiral cord of our kitchen phone wrapped around the island and into the living room, allowing my mom to talk to her friends while we were doing homework or getting ready for bed. She talked to them almost every night, a small circle of women whom I still respect and love. These women bucked the excuses and did friendship in a way that worked for them.

In her quiet, under-the-radar way, I saw my mom fight for friendship in a season that was completely consuming and full.

And the friendships she invested in during that time have lasted for decades.

One friend in particular has become more like a sister to my mom, a second mother to me and my siblings, and a grandmother to all of our kids. She and my mom worked together at the elementary school, both teaching music, and one day they discovered a shared love of cross-stitching. They started having stitching nights at each other's homes a few times a month, the first "girls' nights" I saw my mom participate in.

One summer, my mom was planning a road trip vacation for us, and she invited her friend to join us. She fit right into our minivan and brought buckets filled with freshly baked chocolate chip cookies. We called her Ms. Navigator, as she held the maps and could find her way back to the road after any number of wrong turns. We began traveling together every summer after that, driving cross-country during our summer vacations from school. We did Yellowstone, the Colorado mountains, Boston, and the East Coast, and each trip brought us all closer together.

When my mom was diagnosed with breast cancer, I was a high school senior. Her friend basically moved in to help us all cope and do life. She helped with math homework. She got my mom out of bed to see me in my prom dress. She cooked and cleaned and signed practice charts and read teacher notes. She talked us through the side effects of my mom's cancer treatments and helped us transition together.

Over the years she has helped plan my grandparents' funerals. She's celebrated countless birthdays and holidays with us. She's my youngest child's godmother, promising to help us raise her in faith. She shared her top secret, best-ever, sugar cookie recipe with my middle daughter on her fourth birthday, promising to help her bake up big batches to share (or sneak while Mommy isn't looking!). She's beloved by my son, recalling memories of him as a baby, promising to retell those tales for decades to come. She is as much a part of our family as any of us are.

This is a friend, mother, and aunt in my life whose love has broken the mold, and whom we can all hope to be. One who comes alongside initially as a friend and becomes family along the way. May we all be like her—someone who pours out God's great love, showing up and mothering in whatever way is necessary for those who need it most.

Think about a woman in your life whose love and friendship has broken the mold. Write her a note or pick up the phone to tell her what she means to you!

Reflections

Who has been like a mother to you? What do you love about her?

_____

_____

_____

_____

_____

_____

_____

_____

_____

_____

_____

_____

_____

_____

_____

II. LOVE

While Holding Them Close

Sometimes the sweet moments of motherhood outweigh those of the chaotic variety. Sometimes. But even when the days are long, the messes are serious, the conversations are awkward, and the decisions are difficult, we can dig for the sweetness, for the moments where we hold our children close—no matter how old they are.

These stories are from mothers who hold their children close and their hearts closer. These mothers are doing the constant work of mothering young children, the tongue-biting work of mothering their adult children, and not necessarily treasuring every moment in between. These are the stories of holding our children close and watching God at work.

Grit and Grace

I had three kids in three years. Two months after I had my third child, I realized that within those twelve weeks as a mom of three, I had learned more than I had in all my years. What kinds of things did I learn, you say? Things like the realizations I can do almost anything while nursing a baby, I need less sleep to function than I thought, and friends who bring meals are gold. Now that I'm well beyond the newborn/toddler days and into school age, I can tell you five more lessons I still carry with me to this day:

1. Three kids is no joke.

My husband and I are on constant zone defense—chasing one up the stairs, pulling one off the piano bench before it falls over, and feeding another one—all at the same time. Seriously. And bedtime? Bedtime is like playing whack-a-mole. One kid will go down and another will pop up. The first kid will go back down, and another will get up. This goes on for hours and involves songs, hugs, stories, cups of water, kisses, and all the patience I no longer possess after 7:00 p.m. When my husband and I fall into bed at nigh we are spent, energy and stores of stashed kindness nearly depleted. We draw deep breaths of patience, kindness, joy, gentleness, and peace from God's reserves. Our house is full of dust and life, tiny shoes and books, so much noise and, yeah, so much love.

2. Third-child problems are real.

My firstborn has two baby books, both entirely filled in. My second child has one baby book, partially filled in. My third sweet child has a baby book that remains new in its box. I did fill in her name! Yes, we are saving up for that kid's future counseling.

3. The more kids you have, the more practice you get, which may lead to a more relaxed parenting experience.

When my firstborn was two weeks old, he had a little cold. I scoured the Internet for various childhood diseases, took him to the doctor, and literally lost sleep over his cold. When she was about five weeks old, my third child had her first cold. When she sneezed, I said, "Bless you!" and wiped her nose on my shirt, or hers, whichever had long sleeves. Those two stories, set side-by-side, pretty much sum up the relaxing process of parenting.

4. I've stopped fighting against the rub of mothering.

Several years ago, the word I focused on for the year was *soft*. I still call upon this word when I feel my heart settling into hardening, willing my soul to soften and my flesh to embrace its weakness and need for others. Mothering has forced me to soften. It's provided me three tiny sponges, ready to soak up and absorb whatever I pour out, whether sweet or bitter. It's provided me three tiny mirrors, reflecting the good and the ugly of my actions. It's provided me three tiny humans, rubbing me as sandpaper, and I've found that softening comes more easily when I give into the grit.

Hardness happens when we fight against that which is intended to make us soft.

When he was an infant, my son didn't like to sleep. He fought against it his whole first year of life, with screams and cries and pathetic, red-rimmed eyes peering at me in the dark hours of the night. My heart would break for him, because I knew how much better he'd feel if he only gave in to rest.

It's the same with mothering. As a working mom of three, my life is pulled in many directions—often each one vying for me at the same time. But I'm learning that when I give into the rhythms and demands of my family instead of fighting against them, we're all happier.

5. I am inherently selfish.

I want to steal away and read a good book. I want to eat a hot meal and drink hot coffee, sipping and savoring slow. I want to spend money on impulse buys at Target. I want to sleep in past 7:00 a.m. and take a shower. I want to use the bathroom without little fingers poking under the door (dream big, right?).

But in the season of mothering young kids, I am not able to be selfish. I don't get to put my needs first. I get to love my kids first, and in doing so, I learn to love my God even before them. In this season where selfish is impossible, God draws me closer to His heart and replaces my own wants with His. It's a slow and exhausting process, but the results are pure goodness.

So many lessons from such tiny people. I am so grateful for the One who makes learning them possible only and all by His grace, and for the kids He uses to refine me in the very best ways.

Stay soft, mama.

Reflections

In what ways have you experienced the push and pull—the grit and grace—of mothering young children?

_____

_____

_____

_____

_____

_____

_____

_____

_____

_____

_____

_____

_____

_____

_____

_____

Her children rise up and call her blessed;

her husband also praises her:

"Many women have done noble deeds,

but you surpass them all!"

PROVERBS 31:28–29

Reflections

When they're grown, what do you hope your children say about you? With Proverbs 31 in mind, what kind of woman do you aspire to be?

The Secret to Reaching Hearts

One evening, one of my sweet kids plopped down on our front porch rocker and sighed such a sigh, it sounded as though the whole world would end. I looked into the face of my young adult child and saw weariness, discouragement, and exhaustion. Amidst projects, financial demands, and relationship issues, I knew that life had demanded more than usual and had left this one's soul dry and weary.

I slipped into the kitchen, got a cool drink, crackers, and strong English cheese. I brought out a personal tray and set it next to my depleted child. "How about a shoulder rub for a few minutes?" I asked.

As I put pressure on the knots twisted up from stress, and the drink and snacks were consumed, my child looked at me, breathing out the weariness and said, "I think your great snacks and shoulder rubs have influenced me to love God more than anything else you ever did!"

When God created the world, He did not make us only people of intellect and understanding, but people who had senses that made us feel the touch of a hand, the splendor and taste of a well-cooked meal, the soothing sounds of rain pattering down, music wafting through a room, or the delight of purple mountains amidst fluffy clouds. We are multidimensional beings who are stronger and healthier when all these differing needs are attended to.

As we seek to influence the thoughts, faith, and love of our children, it will be as we do the work of serving, over and over again, of exercising thoughtful and kind deeds, thousands of times, one moment at a time. Someone has to do the work of life that results in pleasurable moments.

And when children are involved, it's often the mama who is the tireless servant, worker, and leader.

To find a model of this servant leadership, we ponder how Christ influenced His own followers. Bending His knee on the hard, dusty floor, His face creased in deep thought, He grabbed a towel. Longing to reach the hearts of His beloved friends, He knelt to touch them, to serve them, to feed them—showing the depths of His love through His gentle, intentional gestures. Only after He had done all this, He began to teach and encourage them.

> *Before the Passover Festival, Jesus knew that his hour had come to depart from this world to the Father. Having loved his own who were in the world, he loved them to the end. . . . Jesus knew that the Father had given everything into his hands, that he had come from God, and that he was going back to God. So he got up from supper, laid aside his outer clothing, took a towel, and tied it around himself. Next, he poured water into a basin and began to wash his disciples' feet and to dry them with the towel tied around him.*
>
> JOHN 13:1–5 (CSB)

Jesus' call to His disciples was compelling—an invitation to lay down their lives, to serve, to experience rejection and even persecution. He was asking them to believe something that would eventually cost each one His life—that He, a carpenter from Nazareth, was actually the Messiah.

The darkness of the evening must have matched His heavy heart. So what did He do before breaking bread and pouring wine, and letting Himself be broken? He washed one hundred and twenty toes. What an example for us as we live life with our children. He has not asked us to do something He has not already done.

Jesus was going to transfer to His disciples the responsibility of taking God's message of redemptive love to the world. But instead of telling them what to do, harshly commanding their allegiance with orders and threats or guilt and manipulative statements, He chose to tie the cords of His heart to theirs with the strong and unbreakable bond of a loving, serving relationship.

Jesus spent His last night on earth with His disciples in service to them. How powerful their memories of that night must have been— the King of the whole universe touching and rubbing their dusty feet and gently drying them with a towel. Their Lord and Master breaking the loaf of bread and serving each of them for the celebrated feast of Passover.

His example of servant leadership set Him apart from all other historical religious leaders. He was not a leader who lorded over His followers and demanded they follow Him. He never coerced their obedience through authoritarianism and fear. Instead, Jesus called them to the excellence of holiness. He lovingly served them in order to win their hearts and show them the means of reaching others' hearts.

Contemplating the hearts of my own children and how I teach them about the grace of God, I realize my love and service to them must come before any of my teaching and training. My time, my attention—even when I'm tired or have other things on my mind—is what builds our relationship and prepares them to listen to what I have to say. Only then, once the wells of their need are filled with the grace of being loved, will my words to them about God's grace finally make sense.

Ultimately, the heart of a leader is to love God, and out of that love, to serve generously as Jesus Himself modeled for us through all the moments of His life.

Reflections

As you ponder your own life, what "acts of service" speak to those you love most? What is one way that a mother or mother-figure has served you?

_____

_____

_____

_____

_____

_____

_____

_____

_____

_____

_____

_____

_____

_____

Why I Don't Treasure Every Moment

"Wherever your treasure is, there the desires of your heart will also be."
LUKE 12:34 (NLT)

"Treasure every moment."

How many times have moms heard this from well-meaning strangers? And how many times have moms gritted their teeth, smiling at that well-meaning stranger while thinking, *I'm not treasuring this particular moment right now!* Often when I hear this phrase, to my ears it translates as, "Never miss one second of your babies growing up or you will miss everything and therefore be a bad mother." Or, "If you don't have warm-fuzzy love each moment of every day of your kids' life, you are a bad mother."

I need the reminder to be present and grateful. To look past the overflowing diaper pail, the toddler melting down because I told him to stop licking the carpet, the baby attached to my hip at all hours of the day. To look beyond the current fleeting moment to the bigger picture. But sometimes the reminders make me question my own heart and bring on guilt. They make me question my gratitude. Was I grateful for the nausea, seven months of sinus infections, bones that wouldn't stay in place, and hemorrhoids? Yes, because we had tried for this baby for years and experienced loss of two pregnancies along the way. I was grateful indeed, but did I treasure these symptoms? Not so much. Sometimes misery is mistakenly substituted for being ungrateful, when in fact those two are not the same thing.

We do this, we mamas. We punish ourselves emotionally with more harshness than anyone else would ever inflict on us. The guilt?

Consuming. The beating ourselves up over an event that happened two months ago? Overwhelming. The way we see ourselves in the mirror? Painful. We heap enough of this guilt onto ourselves; the only thing we need others to heap upon us is grace.

Let me give you a dose of that grace today:

You are released from treasuring every single moment. You have permission to be free of guilt and feel your feelings.

Here is permission to not treasure the moment when you walk into a diaper-less post-nap disaster, when you are physically longing for ten minutes of alone time, or when you just plain want to sleep. Those are hard moments that don't need to be treasured, but that can cause us to lean hard on God's strength (which is a good thing!).

These hard moments, the real and raw ones, the small ones lived in between the big ones, the moments that fall like crumbs between the counter and the stove, leaving our edges frayed? We do not have to tuck them gently into our scrapbooks, lifting them out tenderly in our old age. There are other sweet, special, and priceless moments for tucking away deep into our hearts. But these rough moments are the ones that connect us to God, in prayer and deep breaths and patience. They connect us to our kids, because we understand how difficult moments can sometimes be, and we gain a little empathy. They connect us to each other, because there's a desperate need to know that we're not alone and that we are not bad mothers.

Hug your babies. Comb their hair. Tuck love notes in their lunch. Whisper late-night I love yous into their sleeping ears. Watch them play together. Help them, read to them, snuggle them endlessly. Treasure them. Cherish them. Soak them in.

But the moments? Treasure certain moments while letting go of others, guilt-free. Store the sweet ones in your heart and release the difficult ones to God.

An Invitation to Be Beautiful

I have two daughters, tiny sparkly beauties both. One with dark eyes and a sweet smile and curly pigtails, the other with golden hair feathery straight and eyes blue as the sea. They both light up a room the same way they light up my heart.

When I had my first daughter in the sterile glow of the delivery room, I heard my husband softly say, "It's a girl. A girl." We didn't know before that moment if the baby I'd birth would be a girl or a boy, and in that single second when she was placed on my chest, I breathed deep with both joy and panic.

How do I mother a girl? was the question that burned in my heart. At the time of her birth I had a two-year-old, rough and tumble, sweet and tender, adventurous little boy at home. I was comfortable with being a boy mom. But mothering a girl?

How do you pass along generations of unspoken truth, ancient knowledge stored only in soulful eyes and brief nods, knowing smiles, and a soft pat on the knee?

How do you hand down beauty and passion, drive and ambition, solemnity and care-taking, the feeling of being more than and not enough all at once?

How do I explain to my daughters that women can be the very encouragement that carries us to another day, and women can also be the destroyer of our self-worth?

How do I help my girls see and seek their own deep-seated beauty when I'm still looking for mine?

Years later now, my heart has relaxed as much as our rules. I still worry, but no longer do I panic when thinking about how to teach my daughters what it is to be a woman, because it comes down to this:

We are invited, each of us, to be beautiful.

To see and seek beauty in our everyday, in each other. Our charge is not how to become more beautiful, but to ask instead, *How can I add to the beauty?*

Does this action I'm considering taking add to the beauty of this moment, of this relationship?

Does this conversation with a friend add to the beauty of her heart?

Will this social media post add to the beauty of my life and the lives of others, or is it just filler?

I'm tired of filler. I'm ready to seek beauty.

I want my daughters to grow up on grace-filled beauty, the kind that has been handed down for generations and through friendships, in every casserole dish brought, tissues slid across church pews and movie theater seats, friendships forged, and hearts spurred on to good. I want my daughters to feel beautiful not because of their long eyelashes and silky skin and corkscrew curls, but because of the One who placed beauty deep within their souls—as He did long ago in the Garden.

Eve's story is also ours.

As beauty was lavishly poured like perfume from an alabaster jar, it's ours, this invitation to be beautiful. It's offered straight from the One who created beauty itself, and we can extend it to one another. And that invitation is the glory of grace, of Beauty with a capital B. That invitation is mothering and friendship, and it is healing, vulnerable, and faith-filled.

Together, we can be the beautiful feet that bear good news. Together, we can tell a better, more beautiful story.

Reflections

How can you accept God's invitation to be beautiful? Why is His version of beauty better than the world's? How can you teach this to the children in your life?

_____

_____

_____

_____

_____

_____

_____

_____

_____

_____

_____

_____

_____

_____

_____

Mary and Elizabeth

In those days Mary set out and hurried to a town in the hill country of Judah where she entered Zechariah's house and greeted Elizabeth. When Elizabeth heard Mary's greeting, the baby leaped inside her, and Elizabeth was filled with the Holy Spirit. Then she exclaimed with a loud cry: "Blessed are you among women, and your child will be blessed! How could this happen to me, that the mother of my Lord should come to me? For you see, when the sound of your greeting reached my ears, the baby leaped for joy inside me. Blessed is she who has believed that the Lord would fulfill what he has spoken to her!"

LUKE 1:39–45

Well past childbearing years, Elizabeth bore the cultural shame of barrenness. But the Lord blessed her with a son in a surprising—and miraculous—turn of events. Her years of empty sorrow were filled with much rejoicing.

Likewise, Elizabeth's cousin, Mary, wasn't supposed to have a child either, but for a different reason. Mary wasn't married. Both women, however, experienced the unexpected. Elizabeth became the older woman Mary could turn to during a time of so much uncertainty, welcoming Mary into her home and encouraging her. She knew Mary's child was the Messiah, and her friendship was a beautiful gift to a young, pregnant girl.

It's a wonderful thing to have a friend who understands what you're going through as you enter motherhood! Who is one friend you have that just "gets it"? Reach out and tell her thank you—today! Then consider how you can be that kind of friend to someone else.

Reflections

Who has been a Mary or Elizabeth to you? How can you be that kind of friend to someone else?

_____

_____

_____

_____

_____

_____

_____

_____

_____

_____

_____

_____

_____

_____

_____

_____

A Beautiful Friendship

When I was pregnant with my first, I was equal parts terrified and excited. I didn't have a holy baby inside of me, but I sure felt like the child was God-sent. So at my first ultrasound, when they told me my tiny baby was dead, I was devastated. I felt like shattered glass, my limbs and skin jagged and fragile and raw.

But I had a flicker of hope. I hurried to God's Word and reached out to a girlfriend who stood on His promises.

Your first pregnancy is scary enough, but imagine being Mary—a virgin told by an angel you are going to deliver God in the flesh! That's a little much for anyone to be able to hold together alone. So what does Mary do?

She reaches for a girlfriend who would understand.

Luke writes that Mary "set out and hurried" to the hill country where her relative, Elizabeth, lived. We don't know for sure, but I'm guessing that Mary felt compelled to see Elizabeth because she wasn't quite sure about everything that had happened to her. I can just imagine her thinking, *Did that really happen? Maybe Elizabeth isn't pregnant, and it was all a dream. Or maybe she is pregnant, and it wasn't a dream!*

Mary's emotions must have bounced around inside her heart like a tennis ball. We see her hope, because without Gabriel telling her of Elizabeth's pregnancy, Mary wouldn't have thought of her relative. There were no phones or email to double-check this news. She had to go herself.

It seems that when Mary arrived at Elizabeth's house, she rushed right in, calling out Elizabeth's name. Have you ever been there? Not invited in but needing someone's comfort and connection right away?

My friend was the mother-of-the-bride the weekend I heard about my baby. I was helping at the wedding but couldn't hold my need. I rushed right in and asked her and her family to pray for me and my sweet unborn child.

When Elizabeth heard Mary's greeting, God moved inside her. Yes, it was baby John, the future messenger of God who jumped inside her. But Luke writes that Elizabeth was filled with the Holy Spirit. God's Holy Spirit, who resided in the Holy of Holies, flooded Elizabeth. This was a gift usually reserved for prophets and kings. What an intimate gift from a loving heavenly Father! With the Holy Spirit inside, Elizabeth knew and believed immediately—even without hearing Mary's story—in the Son of God, growing in Mary's womb. Elizabeth, this older woman, with a miracle of her own, spoke life and truth to Mary's young heart.

When my friend and her family placed their hands on me and prayed, I heard truth and life come from her mouth. She prayed that my child would live. Her strong faith spoke to my dwindling spirit, and caused my faith to jump in me.

Mary's response to Elizabeth's faith was to rejoice in the Lord. If she had doubts before, they were gone now. She penned a song to God, championing His power and faithfulness. The Scripture is so specific in the time line, and it seems that Mary stayed to see John's birth. I imagine Elizabeth and Mary over the next few months discussing angelic visitations, sharing their hopes for their sons, and worshipping God as one. I can almost see the two of them—one older, one younger—both with pregnant bellies, laughing and crying together.

What rejoicing there must have been when John was born! The faith of both women likely solidified as they cradled the newborn prophet.

When my daughter was born healthy and normal, despite the doctor's pronouncement, my friend was in the waiting room next to my parents, standing by to see the miracle. And even though we've moved across the country from each other, my heart is knitted to hers. She is the Elizabeth to my Mary. She believed when I only hoped. She spoke life to me and my child. She allowed the Holy Spirit to work through her.

When you're feeling like Mary, and can hardly believe what's happening around you, barge into an older, wiser, more experienced friend's home (or inbox) and ask her to encourage you. Or, if you're older, let a younger woman into your world and point her to the Lord. Remind her of God's promises and plans for her. Show her what God has done for you.

God orchestrated the births of Jesus and John. He chose their mothers, not only for the sake of their babies, but God chose Mary and Elizabeth for each other too. Let's be intentional with our friendships. Let's "set out and hurry" to a girlfriend during the hard, crazy, amazing times. God can, and will, and orchestrate the same kind of Mary-and-Elizabeth relationships for us too.

There's Nothing Balanced about Grace

Many of us—if not most—have bought into a myth, hook, line, and sinker. We spend money on e-courses and books, spend time listening to podcasts and video recordings, and spend energy frantically searching for proof that this myth can in fact be true in our lives.

It eludes us, taunting and teasing and smirking. It tells us that if we don't have it, we never will and we're failures in all that we do. It seems to show up in the lives of others, beckoning us with a wisp of truth then vanishing into thin air as if it never was.

Which it wasn't, because it doesn't exist—even in her life.

Thanks to the parade of perfection on- and off-line, to the culture of doing-it-all without missing a beat, to the perception that everyone else has their ducks in a row (and they're happily marching along in said row), we've managed to convince ourselves that balance is an attainable thing and that, once obtained, it's also sustainable. And that's the lie right there: a perfectly balanced life is the best life.

I just don't think that's true.

It seems to me that if we're doing one thing well, then logically, something else is not being done well. If you think of the very symbol of balance—a two-sided scale—it's no easy task to get it level. It's almost always tipped. And maybe that's the only kind of balance that's maintain-able. But what isn't sustainable or healthy is believing that work and life will balance happily. I don't think they always can, especially for those with a work schedule and young kiddos.

The laundry will always pile up. Same with the dishes and the guilts and the in-a-minutes. We will never be caught up. And this bothers me to the core. I have this picture in my head that one evening, I'll look around the house and at my to-do list, sighing happily and nodding as I think, I'm going to read a book because there's nothing left to accomplish! And then I read a good book in bed sipping a hot cup of tea until I drowsily switch off the lamp.

Yeah . . . Not gonna happen. Like, ever.

Because I have a job. Because I have three kids who make messes, and because I let them. Because words roll their way through my brain and heart and I can't catch them fast enough. Because I love all of the above, and if I focus solely on one thing, the scales tip and all else suffers. Maybe not a lot, but always a little.

Because nothing good is ever finished. There is and will always be more to clean, more to schedule, more to fit in, more to wrap up, more ideas and goals and problems. But the good news is that we can rest in the midst of the undone, knowing that the process is fulfilling in and of itself.

So while balance may be a myth, grace is real and available in spades.

Grace for when our very best falls short.

Grace for when we fall into the trap of comparison.

Grace for the days we'd rather be with our kids.

Grace for the days we'd rather be at work.

Grace for using a too-small diaper because we ran out again.

Grace for the days that go by without bathing our kids—or ourselves.

Grace for our "meals" being made up of scraps off our kids' plates or treats smuggle-eaten behind the pantry door.

Grace for the friends who don't reply to our text, and grace for when we are that friend.

Grace for days, people—grace for eternity. Chances are good I will never live out that scene in my head where I go to sleep, satisfied smile on my face because that to-do list is complete. But every day we have the chance to live out a far better reality. We can lay our heads down, a grin playing on our lips because we gave it a go and God was there—knowing we get to do it again tomorrow while holding our kids close and teaching them what it looks like to live a faithfully un-balanced life.

Reflections

What does grace look like in your life? What can you embrace or let go
of in order to live a "faithfully un-balanced" life?

_____

_____

_____

_____

_____

_____

_____

_____

_____

_____

_____

_____

_____

_____

_____

_____

_____

_____

_____

The Worst Kind of Mommy War

After having three kids in less than four years, I weighed more than ever before. I wore a bigger size than ever before. My tummy had more soft folds than ever before. Sometimes I didn't recognize my own face in the mirror or photographs.

Other women with young kids? They're also softer. They've gained tummy folds and a little jiggle too. They've cried in dressing rooms when they see the numbers on tags sewn into garments, and they've said things about themselves in their heads that they'd never repeat out loud or say to another woman. When they confess these things to me, I can't believe it, because to me, those women are truly beautiful. This is how I know that the worst mommy war is the one we wage on ourselves.

And why? Why do we declare war with our bodies, with our very beings?

Listen, the size listed on a tag does not—cannot—define you. That soft, gently squishy stomach grew people and cares for them deeply. Thighs that touch speak to a strong body that carries more than the weight of itself; it carries the hopes and fears of a whole family.

For all of these reasons and so many more, it's time to declare peace with your body. To be kind to it. To whisper a thanks to your waistline for a job well done. To feed it well, to water it often, to clothe it with joy, and to give it rest.

I'll never forget the day my preschool-age son barreled into the office where I was working away, clutching a bouquet of flowers from the grocery store. He'd picked it out himself while he was out shopping with daddy, telling him, "I have to get Mommy these pretty flowers!" He thinks I'm as beautiful as those blooms.

I know he thinks this, because I've always thought my own mother is beautiful.

Your children think you're beautiful. God fashioned you exactly as He pictured you in His mind. You are fearfully and wonderfully made, just like your kids are. We believe that for them, don't we? We can believe it for us, too.

Let these be the measurements that matter. When we do, we win the war.

For you created my inmost being;

you knit me together in my mother's womb.

I praise you because I am fearfully and wonderfully made;

your works are wonderful,

I know that full well.

PSALM 139:13–14 (NIV)

Reflections

What ways do you wage war on yourself? What is one way you can treat yourself with kindness this week?

_____

_____

_____

_____

_____

_____

_____

_____

_____

_____

_____

_____

_____

_____

_____

_____

III. *Love*
and Laundry

Dishes and laundry. Carpool and the 9-to-5 grind. Sweeping the kitchen and wiping the countertops. Sippy cups and dentist appointments. Grocery shopping and homework helping. Walking the dog and washing the car.

Much of motherhood—at any age, in any stage—is built of and on our mundane, everyday tasks. We can get bogged down in this kind of doing, or we can choose to see God's glory amidst it. That's right—God's glory shines in the messiest of kitchens, the crumb-iest of minivans, the darkest middle-of-the-night feedings, the earliest drives to before-school practice, and the emptiest hallways of lonely hearts. It's often in the ordinary, everyday tasks and places where God speaks to our hearts and where we can accept the peace only He can give.

Read on for stories of the extraordinary ordinary, the glory in the mess, the commonplace cornerstones of real-life mothering, and the way God shows up in it all.

#RealMomConfessions

When I was four years into motherhood, I wrote a post on Facebook and shared a few confessions from my recent mothering. That week, my confessions included:

- Not only did I let my daughter eat crackers off the floor, I put them there for her in the first place because all of the bowls were in the dishwasher.

- The pile of dishes in my sink was so high that I honestly couldn't see my kids on the other side of them.

- My kids no longer played "kitchen" with their play kitchen. They played "coffee shop drive-through," offering "vanilla lattes" through the little window.

I pressed post and went on my way, back into diapers and laundry and work and being up to my elbows in children. Hours later after bedtime, I opened my laptop and was floored to see dozens of comments from other moms sharing their real confessions too. I've continued posting these #realmomconfessions for years, and the moms keep showing up.

Moms have shared the number of days between baths for their kids. They've shared how many meals from the drive-through were eaten that week in the van. They have shared how frustrated and exhausted they were. They've shared their laundry mountains. They have asked for prayer as they returned to work from maternity leave and made difficult decisions for their children. They've shared their loneliness and craving for friendship. And along with their battle stories, they have shared their victorious, cheerful, and funny stories too.

They have shared their real confessions of mothering, and they've changed me. Because of them and their brave sharing of stories, I am a less judgmental woman. My first reactions have shifted; they contain more grace and love than I ever could've mustered on my own. God has used these confessions to keep me humble (the only possible response upon finding out that you're in the showering frequency minority) and to keep me plugged in to the needs of those around me.

Real moms are the best kind. The kind of mom who doesn't hide behind the façade of perfection but instead embraces her imperfections? The kind of mom who knows she has but a moment to pray, so she grabs hold of just the right words to offer earnestly? The kind of mom whose kids know she—and they—can laugh at mistakes, welcome grace from each other, and make things right with a sincere apology and the promise of new mercy each morning? That's my kind of real mom.

Sharing the real moments of mothering with other moms has changed me, it's changed how I see other moms, and it's changed how I view my failures.

Because in confessing our shortcomings, God redeems that which we've deemed failure.

When a mom confesses her shame at going through the drive-through again, and another mom chimes in her support and love of waffle fries and a big sweet tea? Redemption.

When a mom confesses her fear of returning to work after maternity leave, worried about juggling work and kids and new baby and laundry and all the things, and another mom tells her to breathe? Assures her that it will be okay, that she will make it, that she can—even should—ask for help? Redemption.

When a mom confesses and others support her, it's glory in mess.

Jesus—the One birthed by a young mom and placed in a dirt and straw-filled manger?—Jesus understands this kind of glory, the kind that's sometimes hidden in the mess. God is all about the messy glory; in fact, I'm convinced He kind of loves it. And mamas? We live there, in that space where the glorious ordinary meets the extraordinary every day.

When we come together to share in that place of cracker crumbs and trembling fear of messing up our kids, hearts overwhelmed at the thought of another day and sticky fingers all up in our faces? That's when we know there can be—there has to be—real community in mothering. We must cling to loving and supporting each other well.

What a world it would be if we not only gave another mom the benefit of the doubt, but erased the doubt in the first place.

So that thing you'd confess if you only could? Friend, God already knows it and is ready to redeem it. Let go of any shame, embarrassment, or doubt! You are a good mom—a real, good mom—and God is making you even better.

Reflections

Do you have any "real mom confessions"? Write them down here, laugh, and give thanks!

_____

_____

_____

_____

_____

_____

_____

_____

_____

_____

_____

_____

_____

_____

_____

_____

Choosing to Thrive

Do not be conformed to this age, but be transformed by the renewing of your mind, so that you may discern what is the good, pleasing, and perfect will of God.

ROMANS 12:2

For the first ten years of my faith journey, my understanding of the Bible was dependent on Sunday school classes and small group studies. My prayer time was more like sending a text message to God when I urgently needed something. All that changed when one of my best friends called me out on my commitment to God. She said, "I'm concerned that God is nothing more than an item on your to-do list. If you really want to grow in your faith, you need to give Him your time, not just your demands."

She was right. Like a clumsy toddler learning how to walk, I began a habit of meeting with God each day. As soon as my daughters went down for their afternoon nap, I headed for the couch and read my Bible—closing my eyes to the laundry, dishwasher, and emails beckoning my attention. Within months, I could see fruit from the dedication of this time, and I felt closer to the Lord.

Over the next few years, I moved my quiet time to the mornings and committed to reading the whole Bible. It took three grace-marked years. Now when I look upon that worn-down Bible, I feel the warmth of God's love and mercy, knowing it was His sustaining power that enabled me to accomplish such a feat as a young mama nursing her twins and chasing them through their toddler years.

I remember dreaming of the day when all the kids would head off to school and I would finally have uninterrupted, unrushed hours with the Lord. If only. Instead of oodles of time, I came upon oodles of demands on my time. When all my children finally entered school and I found myself finally alone, I filled my schedule to the brim. Like a racehorse let out of the gates, I began to feel like I must sprint through each minute, especially if I was going to complete the "must-do" tasks.

Yes, I was committed to giving God a portion of my time, but my heart was numbing out. God ended up back on my checklist of things to do each day, and I could sense the damage to my spiritual life. Even though I spent one or two mornings a week with God, it wasn't enough. I was feeling more and more parched. I knew I needed more than what I was getting—and giving—to God.

I was desperate for change and remembered what my friend once challenged me to do—to get into the Word. I want to be that friend for you. In Romans 12, Paul encourages us to renew our minds. We do this through time in God's Word. I've learned the hard way what can happen when I neglect to spend time each day with Him. As I steep myself in Scripture, I see God move in my life. I go from parched to refreshed, from despairing to humbly redirected, from striving to thriving.

And so can you.

Moses answered the people,

"Do not be afraid.

Stand firm and you will see the deliverance

the L<small>ORD</small> *will bring you today. . . .*

The L<small>ORD</small> *will fight for you; you need*

only be still."

EXODUS 14:13–14 (NIV)

Reflections

How can you steep yourself in God's Word? What fruits do you see
growing as a result of spending time with Him?

_____

_____

_____

_____

_____

_____

_____

_____

_____

_____

_____

_____

_____

_____

_____

The Holiness of Slow

"You're so busy!" was a phrase I heard often. Each time someone said it, usually accompanied by a little nervous laughter, my smile would falter for a moment before I replied. I realized that I must have been wearing stress like a badge of honor.

When I walked into a room, I'd be huffing and puffing, rolling my eyes at the circus act that it took to bring three kids anywhere. I'm usually a sweaty mess because I have three bags to carry, three car seats to unbuckle, three jackets to zip kids into, six shoes to Velcro or tie, a double stroller to set up—and I'm just one mom juggling it all. But I was no different than any other mom of tiny children, and most of my friends seemed much calmer when arriving.

I'd hustle us from home to preschool to drive-through to home, and from task to task to task once we were at home. Our days didn't include more than part-time preschool, kindergarten, and church, but it was more than enough once we added in meals, snacks, laundry, vacuuming up dog hair, getting people dressed, packing lunches, work, and all the other daily items that cropped up.

My to-do list was owning my heart. I was happy with the amount that I'd accomplish, yet I still felt like I hadn't quite completed enough because of the tasks remaining. Often left on that list were my own well-being (like many women, I put myself last), cooking good meals (I wasn't taking the time to make any kind of plan), and feeling like I hadn't spent enough time truly being present with my kids. That list of leftovers was giving me anxiety, overshadowing any peace from the items I'd actually checked off.

I was stretching myself like Mrs. Incredible—except real people aren't made from elastic, and when stretched too thin, we snap. It had been months since I'd lived out my favorite scene—a steaming cup of cinnamon tea, my trusty old armchair, and a good book in my hands— because it felt self-indulgent. There was always more to accomplish; refreshing my heart wasn't high on the to-do list.

I had begun sacrificing the holiness of ordinary, everyday moments for hustled minutes, and I was not okay with that. I realized that slow is holy and that everything holy and ancient and worthwhile is slow:

Cooking real food

Cleaning well

Growing babies

Planting a garden

Changes of seasons

Changes of heart

All holy. All ancient. All worthwhile. All slow. Not a single one of them is something that can be hurried up or hustled through.

This is no accident. God has not called us to rush and hurry and hustle through our days. He's called us to be still. In so many words, in so many Scriptures:

- Psalm 23 promises that He will lead us beside still waters and faithfully restore our souls.

- Psalm 46:10 implores us to be still and to know that He alone is God.

- Exodus 14:14 declares that if we are still, He will fight for us.

- First Samuel 12:16 bids us to stand still so we can see what He's going to do.

- Psalm 37:7 reminds us to be still and wait patiently for Him, even as others seem to be succeeding and moving ahead of us.

Since having these realizations, I've extracted myself from the hurried life I was living (and forcing onto my family). I've cleared space on the calendar, making room for friends and family and grace. When feasible, I'm writing fewer to-dos on my task list. I'm reconciling my desire for a badge of honor in busyness with what God says is honorable. That's what I'm aiming for these days. I'm drinking more water and eating good food, bumping God's command for me to take care of the body He gave me a notch higher on the list. We're taking walks through the neighborhood as a family, reading more books at bedtime, and enjoying our time together. And I'm drinking tea in my armchair again.

This didn't happen overnight; it's taken a lot of time and intention. The siren song of a full calendar still sings, but its promises are empty and hollow. And now I know deep in my bones that with an emptier calendar or task list comes a fulfilled heart. At the end of the day, when I close my eyes and let my head hit the pillow, I no longer care about what's left on my to-do list. All that's left hanging over my head is love.

May we give God the space to do what He can only accomplish in our stillness. May we heed His call to be still. May we welcome rest and lean into the holiness of slow.

Reflections

How can you give God space to do His work in your stillness?

_____

_____

_____

_____

_____

_____

_____

_____

_____

_____

_____

_____

_____

_____

_____

Rest Is Best

"Rest is best, rest is best!" My kids love this little song from the PBS show *Daniel Tiger.* The show is modeled after Mr. Rogers, and you can hear it in the lyrics of the brief songs that the calm, patient, and kind adults sing. This particular song has several applications: when you're crabby, rest is best. When you're sick, rest is best. When you're overwhelmed, rest is best.

As a mom, I need to sing this one on repeat.

It's easy to both burn the midnight oil and wake up with the sun when you've got little kids underfoot. There's always something more to get done!

Moms don't get a lot of rest. Often, we even forget that God promises rest. Real rest. The kind that allows us to catch our breath, to laugh, to feel peaceful.

It may be hard to find pockets of peace during our crazy days, but you can creatively make space to experience His peace. Create moments for rest amidst your day, squishing them in and around your regular happenings. Pray in the preschool pickup line. Read or write the Word during your lunch break. Hop in the shower and take a few minutes to lay your heart before the Lord while the water runs (and your kids enjoy a snack and show). Get creative, and make rest work for you.

You can do this, and you will be all the better for resting in His presence.

The Lord replied, "My Presence will go with you, and I will give you rest." EXODUS 33:14 (NIV)

Take Real Care of Your Real Self

"Self-care" has become a cultural buzzword. Unfortunately, I've observed that while the importance of and need for actual self-care has increased, our self-care tools have decreased in their helpfulness.

Because when we think we're practicing self-care, often we're actually practicing self-indulgence. Real self-care is not selfish. It's not a waste of time. It's not pedicures. It's not scrolling Facebook. It's not shopping online. It's not chocolate.

Self-care is not self-indulgence. So how do we take real care of our real selves?

God has given us a plan for exactly this.

Think about the best mom you know. Maybe it's your mom. Maybe it's a woman at your church. If you went to her in a frazzled and overwhelmed state, what would she tell you to do to take care of yourself?

Most likely, she would make sure you're comfortable on the couch, maybe with a fuzzy blanket.

She'd get you a drink of water.

Or she might advise you to take a shower.

Go to sleep.

Turn off the TV. Put down the phone. Close the laptop.

Invite a friend over.

Wear clean clothes.

Laugh.

Read a book.

Eat food that helps your body. And have dessert.

Forgive yourself. Forgive the other person.

This amazing parent? This is someone that God can be for us.

This is one way God wants to care for us, like the best parent there ever was. Ready with relaxation and/or a kick in the pants to shake it off and get going. Because let's be honest—sometimes that's the combination we actually need!

He has counted the hairs on our heads. Psalm 139 says:

> *How precious are your thoughts about me, O God. They cannot*
> *be numbered!*
> *I can't even count them; they outnumber the grains of sand!*
> (vv. 17–18 NLT)

God thinks of us more often than there are grains of sand. How amazing! God truly cares for us, and He'd like us to care for ourselves, too. He's given us a glimpse of how to do that.

One way we can care for ourselves is to rest, to pause and breathe and slow down and rest. And God? He rested. God paused.

After working really hard, God took a breather.

It's the first example of good and godly rest we see in Scripture. In the first chapter of Genesis, God has just created everything. Everything! And then the second chapter opens with Him finishing up His work and resting. Genesis 2:2 says:

By the seventh day God had finished the work He had been doing; so on the seventh day he rested from all his work. Then God blessed the seventh day and made it holy, because on it he rested from all the work of creating that he had done. (vv. 2–3 NIV)

Mothers work hard. Mothers basically run the world. But has anyone ever worked harder than the Creator of the world? The Maker of all things? No. And the Creator took rest. God recognized the hard work He'd done after making everything in the world, including the first humans, and He paused when He was finished.

And it's a good thing He did, because next He'd have to deal with Adam and Eve's rebellion.

This. Is. Huge. *God rests before He cares for His children.*

The rest of Genesis chapter 2 is all about how God plants the garden of Eden, prepares it for Adam and Eve, teaches them about caring for the Earth, introduces Adam to the animals, and creates Eve. Then in the next chapter, everything falls apart when they eat that forbidden fruit.

This is a game changer. God works really hard, and then God rests before He cares for His disobedient children.

This is what God has modeled for us. Is it what we are modeling for our kids?

That old airplane analogy serves us well. During the announcements given before a flight, flight attendants remind passengers to "place an oxygen mask on yourself before assisting others."

While it goes against our own tendencies, we actually do need our own oxygen before we can be of any good to someone else. But as parents, there is nothing we wouldn't do for our kids—including depriving ourselves of that which is life-giving. This is why we need the flight reminder, and why we need to read and re-read what God shows us back in Genesis.

Rest is a form of true and godly self-care, and this is what God models so well, right at the beginning of His Word.

As we discover the ways we need to care for ourselves, doing something we enjoy is usually low on the to-do list. We always have too many tasks to finish to devote time to things we love doing, right?

Maybe not.

I grew up with two younger siblings and a single mom. She worked two jobs—she was a teacher and the choir director at our church—which did not leave much spare time for self-care. But she did the best she could with what she had, as we all do, and this was one practice she made time for.

She would cross-stitch. She worked every night on a piece, crafting enough of them to decorate our home and to gift at Christmas to her parents and friends. She worked diligently, carefully, on each stitch while sitting in the blue velvet chair under the brightest lamp in the house so she could see the tiny stitches in her cloth. She still stitches in that chair, under that lamp, and I proudly display each piece she's given me in my home.

Besides her stitching time, I don't remember my mom ever focusing on herself in another way.

She taught me that the things you love matter. Doing something you love, that you love, is important—even worth giving up sleep for sometimes.

May you care for yourself in godly, thoughtful, intentional, and life-giving ways.

May you give your children the legacy gift of care-filled habits.

And may you grow together toward the love that draws us in, shows us how to care for ourselves and others, and promises rest.

Trusting God with All Your Heart

The staircase is dark and looming to a two-year-old. Her little feet push upward, but her pudgy hand can't reach the light switch. With the kind of determined, stubborn bravery found only in toddlers, she chooses to climb the staircase in the dark, deciding that reaching her goal is worth the moments of fear. Her final target, waiting at the top of the stairs in the light? Mommy.

My brave girl wasn't the only one navigating a darkened path during that time. That season was one of living in limbo. Our home had sold, and we—a family of five plus a dog—moved into my mother's townhome. We were living on top of one another with boxes and people underfoot. We submitted offer after offer on homes in the area, and each one was passed over for another. With each offer, we asked God to lead and guide our path to a new home. And isn't that how we could pray every day? That in following Him, He would guide us Home?

After seven offers had been submitted, my trust was faltering. Would God indeed take care of us? Would we be in our own home by my kids' birthdays? By Christmas? By the next year? I had no idea, but every day we weeded out more options and it felt like we were making room for God's path to widen, inch by inch.

Trusting God with all of our hearts doesn't mean He will wrap up the job like we think He should, neat and tidy with a bow on top. If I'd had my way, we'd have been in a new home the day after we closed on our old one. But that's not how it shook out. We ended up living with my mom for three months before the seventh offer we submitted was the first one to be accepted. We moved into that new house with great joy, let me tell you.

Trusting God with all our hearts means leaning on His understanding, knowing that whatever it is, His plan is enough, His plan is good, and all will be well. Those months living in such close quarters with my mom had their own kind of difficulty, but they also brought us all together in an irreplaceable way. She and my husband grew closer, and she bonded with our kids in a way that can only happen when living ordinary life together.

Trusting God with all our hearts doesn't mean answers will come swiftly, or even at all. I don't understand everything, and I sometimes question the path He leads me down. But trusting God with all our hearts means we rely on and trust in God's own understanding of His plan. It means we trust that God understands the how and why. It means we know that we don't need to know everything; God does.

Trusting God with all our hearts and thinking of Him in all our ways means opening our hearts to His path, scary and new and untraveled as it may be. It means stepping forward in faith, taking one stair at a time until we're safe at the top, the darkness behind us.

When we're not sure how to trust, we lean hard and step forward in faith, knowing that God is waiting at the top to welcome us with outstretched arms.

*Trust in the L*ORD *with all your heart,*

and do not rely on your own understanding;

in all your ways know him,

and he will make your paths straight.

PROVERBS 3:5–6

Reflections

What is one area in which you trust God with all your heart? How can you grow your trust in Him in other areas?

Surrender and Seek

It was everything I dreamed of, and absolutely nothing I could have imagined. I opened my eyes, popped straight up in my bed, and sat quietly as the tears began to stream down my cheeks. I had everything I'd prayed for—healthy children, a wonderful husband, a house, great friends, and family. On that morning, however, I looked around my bedroom and felt completely overwhelmed by my own reality. I felt grateful yet lost, content yet empty, and confused by this increasingly awkward array of emotions.

I was a mom of four young girls, and I was overcome by the responsibilities that accompanied raising them. From the car we drove, to the house we lived in, and the dinners I prepared, nothing felt right. I was convinced I was not enough.

I sat in bed alone, listening to my husband prepare breakfast. I could hear my six-year-old singing her new favorite song, my four-year-old crying over a lost sock, and my twin two-year-olds running around covered in finger paint. I wondered how I got there and whose life I was living. More than that, I questioned who was in control of it all.

Now, don't get me wrong. I loved my family and my life. I knew I needed to trust God with my life, but how? I knew He was always with me, but why did I feel lonely? I knew He was my joy, but why was I so sad?

Everything around me seemed to be spinning out of control. The physical, emotional, and financial burdens of motherhood had replaced the faith, trust, and joy I once knew were mine.

The longer I sat in tears, the more I could tell that something was changing. It was not my situation, but my focus and perspective. With each tear that fell, I finally gave up. Unknowingly, I reached the end of my fight for control. My will, my power, my strength, and my efforts were not working. As a result, I gave God the freedom to be Lord of my life in reality, not just in lip-service.

I surrendered to Jesus' words found in Matthew 6:25–34:

> *"Therefore I tell you: Don't worry about your life, what you will eat or what you will drink; or about your body, what you will wear. Isn't life more than food and the body more than clothing? Consider the birds of the sky: They don't sow or reap or gather into barns, yet your heavenly Father feeds them. Aren't you worth more than they? Can any of you add one moment to his life span by worrying? And why do you worry about clothes? Observe how the wildflowers of the field grow: They don't labor or spin thread. Yet I tell you that not even Solomon in all his splendor was adorned like one of these. If that's how God clothes the grass of the field, which is here today and thrown into the furnace tomorrow, won't he do much more for you—you of little faith? So don't worry, saying, 'What will we eat?' or 'What will we drink?' or 'What will we wear?' For the Gentiles eagerly seek all these things, and your heavenly Father knows that you need them. But seek first the kingdom of God and his righteousness, and all these things will be provided for you. Therefore don't worry about tomorrow, because tomorrow will worry about itself. Each day has enough trouble of its own."*

I stopped trying to escape, fix, and re-create the life He had placed before me, and I finally gave Christ the freedom to control and use my life in the here and now.

Maybe, like me, you know God's Word but you're trying to see His face through the worry. God does not aimlessly remind us of His ability to provide. Instead, He gives specific direction on how to rest in His provision.

Seek Him.

I wish I could tell you that everything changed after I wiped my tears and surrendered. It was the beginning of a new me, a me that God could use because I laid my anxieties at His feet and placed my hands in His. Now, years later, I still have my moments of worry. I find myself having to lay it all down again, but I also find that each time it gets a little easier.

Replacing personal worry with seeking His Kingdom is a daily surrender. Are you wondering how you ended up in this place—out of control and overwhelmed by your dreams, your emotions, your marriage, or your family? Today, remember that you can't have victory in your life while operating in your own sufficiency. Today, whether you're in a position that the world would consider a crisis, or you're in a situation that looks just fine from the outside, I encourage you to get desperate and "give up."

Surrender. Seek Him. Lay it down. And watch Christ pick you up.

Reflections

Are there areas of your life that cause you anxiety? How can you lay
those anxieties before God today?

_____

_____

_____

_____

_____

_____

_____

_____

_____

_____

_____

_____

_____

_____

_____

_____

IV. LOVE

While Letting Them Fly

When I was growing up, at times my mother referred to me as "her little bird." She didn't mean I was petite or dainty; she meant I was headstrong and stubborn, insisting on flying into a window over and over rather than giving up in defeat.

Not the most flattering depiction of my personality, but it was accurate. My mom let me fly. She gave me permission to live into the person God created me to be, mistakes and all, and she encouraged my flight.

This section includes stories of flying. Of letting go. Of trusting the One who gave us children and mothers. These are stories of graduation, of grown kids leaving home, of the process and resolve it takes to let them fly. These are stories of holding dreams loosely, eventually letting them fly. And these are stories of parents who journey home to heaven as we hold their hands, letting their souls fly home.

Some stories are sweet. Some stories are sad. All of them point to God's grace, goodness, and love, and the hope we can find in the letting go.

Back-to-School

God stands with us in the aisles of picked-over school supplies. In the middle of the living room, surrounded by labels yet to be stuck on dozens of those school supplies. In the college dorm room, which was empty when we arrived and which, now as we drive away, is crammed with instant mac and cheese, twin extra-large comforters, and our whole heart. At the bus stop, waiting for the very first time.

God stands with us, and He stands with our kids as they fly.

We've worked, prepared, packed, and prayed for these days. The backpacks are full. The lunches are packed. Alarm clocks are set, and outfits laid out. Bags have been stuffed, books have been bought, and forms (so. many. forms.) have been filled out.

Some of us are elated. Some of us are fearful. Some of us are teary. Most of us are all of the above.

It does my heart good to remember that God goes first, especially into the places where parents cannot. He goes before. He's ready and waiting for our kids. They do not walk through those doors alone.

I find myself questioning what more I can send with my kids into school to give them peace, love, assurance, and confidence. If I read that book to them, they'll remember. If I send a note in their lunch, they'll remember. If I go with them to college and move into their dorm with them, they won't be able to forget. But the only One who can accompany our kids and provide everything they need is standing by them already. With our love tucked in their hearts and God by their sides, we have done all that we can do to prepare our kids for going back to school.

We'll hold their hands while walking into the big brick buildings, while leading them to the homeschool tables, and while walking them into their dorms. We hold their hands, and then we will let their hands go, knowing that all the while, He will hold them close.

Reflections

How can (or did) you make the first day of school special for your kids without stressing yourself out?

_____

_____

_____

_____

_____

_____

_____

_____

_____

_____

_____

_____

_____

_____

_____

_____

To Train Up a Child

In the years between the momentous day a tiny, helpless infant enters your world and the emotional day when your child—now a young man or young woman—strikes off on their own, it's not only the child who will grow and transform, but the mother too. Some stages of parenthood are more physical, like the sleep-deprivation of new motherhood or the exhaustion of chasing toddlers, and some are more emotional, like dealing with hormonal teenagers or high school graduations.

Five of our eight children have grown up and moved out, and I can tell you, it doesn't get any easier. I dread graduation years; everything within me pushes back against the thought of them. We're in the middle of a six-year period when our four youngest children will all graduate, and I'm already bracing myself for the spring they're all gone.

Seeing other parents embrace their children's graduations—even get excited about them—tells me my reaction isn't necessarily the norm. Why do I feel this way? Part of it is an end-of-an-era feeling: when you've mothered a child so long, it's hard to step back and accept they don't need you in the same ways they did before. But really, I think it's more than that. It's a fear that I didn't prepare my child to capably handle life on their own, to continue their education or get the job they want, and to firmly stand for what's right no matter (or in spite of) what the world says.

Last year, my nineteen-year-old daughter joined a group of young women on a three-month trip to Central America with the World Race Semesters program. They spent one month in each of three locations, serving the local communities. As excited as I was for her and the opportunity she had, I spent more of the time before she left in fear for her health and safety than in anticipation of how she might bless those she'd meet.

It was my sweet friend Joy who helped put it into perspective when she left me the following message:

"I want you to be encouraged that this is what you've worked toward so hard all these years, as you and the Lord created her and taught her and molded her into who He's made her to be. And this is what you did all that for: so that she could go off into the world and do amazing things."

So that she could go off into the world and do amazing things—isn't that what we want for our children?

I had forgotten the words I've told other moms over the years: God has a plan for our children, and it's between Him and them. We will not derail or destroy it. It doesn't hinge on our successes or failures.

It's not about us.

As moms, we will never fully prepare our children for what lies ahead when they leave our nests. How could we? But if we raise them with purpose, instilling a foundation of biblical values, and with the objective to be good, kind people who shine God's light wherever they go, then they will be world-changers no matter the path they take.

Train up a child in the way he should go:

and when he is old, he will not depart from it.

PROVERBS 22:6 (KJV)

Reflections

What hopes do you have for the children you love?

_____

_____

_____

_____

_____

_____

_____

_____

_____

_____

_____

_____

_____

_____

_____

_____

_____

Eighteen Summers

My son's birthday is always on the first day of summer, June 21. He is our third and last child, our first boy. He was our straggler child, joining the family nine summers after his sisters. But he was chosen. Prayed for. Wanted at that exact moment in time.

I worried about having a boy because I thought of myself as a girl mom. I didn't know a thing about being a boy mom. I thought boys were about bugs and snakes, and I wasn't at all experienced with those sorts of things. Silly me. God just smiled on me and nudged my heart not to worry. You'll adore him, bugs and all, and he'll adore you, inexperience and all. You are the right mom for him, you'll see.

He was an adorable, curly-headed blond boy with a mischievous grin and the biggest brown eyes you ever did see. While he was strong and independent, he was still a mama's boy. When he was just a few years old, he sobbed on my shoulder after discovering I was already married to his daddy and he'd have to find his own wife someday. I held him tenderly and treasured that moment, knowing I would smile really big about it when he was a teen and realized I wasn't quite as wonderful as he assumed in childhood.

Eighteen summers of childhood is all we get, and they fly by quickly when you are raising kids to be adults.

Family life is busy and full and crazy. Memories of sand in toes and diapers and hair will blur into memories of waving good-bye to a brave boy through a mama's tears at the summer camp drop-off.

I knew all along that I needed to soak in each moment as it happened. I knew I needed to bask in the summers filled with bike riding, scraped knees, treasure hunts, sprinklers, water guns, ice cream cones, beach trips, basketball, playing in the park, backyard campouts with his dogs and his dad, and family s'mores around the fire pit, because the bittersweet truth is those days never seem like nearly enough when you look back on just eighteen summers, quickly becoming a memory of days gone by.

Now that the curly-headed boy has turned into a strong handsome teen, I brace myself knowing full well the days ahead will sometimes feel painfully long. But you figure out after raising two teens already that the days will not always feel nearly long enough. Eighteen years isn't enough to get a boy ready to be a man, let alone enough time to prepare to be a mama to let him go.

But you do the best you can. Some days you just fall on your knees and pray for his soul and his steps because even though you know your role as his protector will evolve as fast as you witnessed those little boy shoulders broaden and squeaky adorable voice deepening, you will always, always be his fiercely protective but soft-hearted mama. Your heart is head over heels for this boy, even when he doesn't see it or want to believe it. He is your earthly treasure to have and to hold and to eventually let go.

Sometimes through tears and sometimes through laughter you thank God that He gave this gift to you.

You just want to hold that little boy a little tighter while you learn to gently let him go. You pray for God's grace and mercy as you raise your boy-turned-young-man up with arms wide open, entrusting who he is and will become to the One who loves him more.

We have eighteen summers of childhood. That thought leaves me a little weak in the knees, so I want to cherish each and every moment of the summers we have left.

I sometimes pray for that day when he may kneel before God at the altar to ask another girl to be his wife. I'll know I'll look over at him and wink through teary eyes as I let him go. But until that day, I'll soak up each summer and day we have together (while we work on taking out the trash without reminders, and other habits for which I know his wife will someday thank us). Until that day, I will treasure this one.

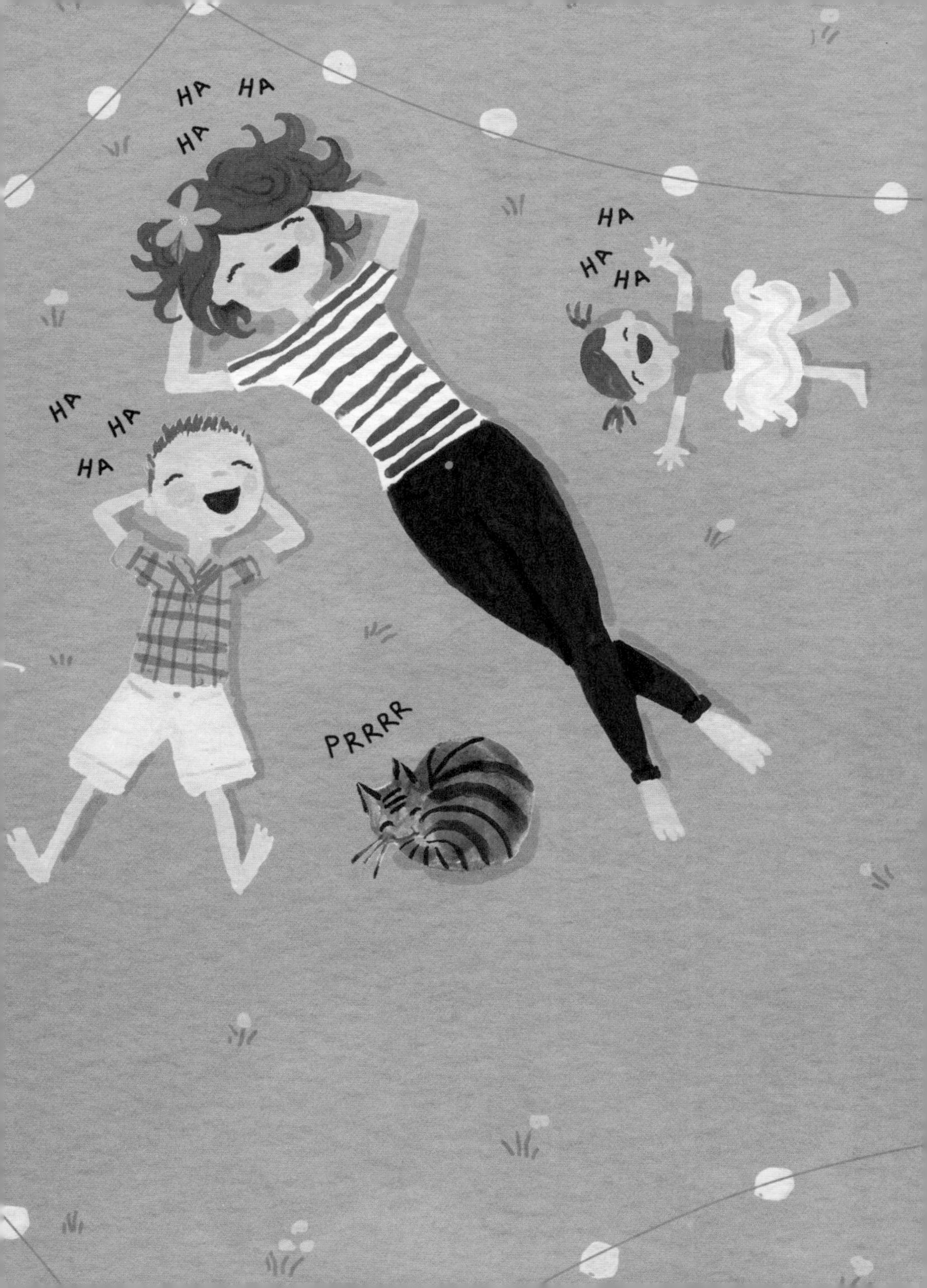
HA HA
HA
HA
HA HA
HA
HA
HA
PRRRR

When It's Time to Send

There is a time for crying and laughing,
weeping and dancing . . . for embracing and parting.
There is a time for finding and losing,
keeping and giving away.

ECCLESIASTES 3:4–6 (CEV)

I blame it on Fuji apples. My heart was glass, teetering on the edge of a shelf, poised to shatter whenever the world tilted. I just couldn't predict when the ground would sway.

Because I had thought I was fine, my guard was down; I was just grocery shopping, after all. When I rounded the produce corner that morning, I wasn't expecting a body blow, but there they were, red and speckled with flecks of green. I lost it right then and there in the fruit section of Publix. Fuji apples were her favorite.

My daughter and firstborn was about to graduate. The entire school year was a succession of lasts, and somehow, I had been able to steel my heart and steady myself for the "big" things. But when I least expected it, when I wasn't paying careful attention, something would find its way in through a tiny crevice and leave me in a puddle.

Fuji apples, for goodness' sake.

Motherhood is a million tender moments. We celebrate one first after another—steps or teeth or haircuts or school. We are thrilled for every success of our children. We anguish over any heartache or injury or injustice. We carry our babies for nine months, and though they may physically leave our bodies, a part of them remains. Sometimes our hearts carry the heaviest load. We devote ourselves to bringing them up in the discipline and instruction of the Lord (Eph. 6:4), but the hard and best reality is one day they will leave. That is good and healthy and right.

Motherhood is ever bittersweet.

First, holding tightly.

Then, carrying with an open hand.

Finally, letting go.

Men may have physical strength of steel, but women are emotional titanium.

We celebrate with you, sweet sisters, the mamas who are on this cusp of sending—a firstborn, a last born, or maybe one in the middle. Those of us who've gone before you and felt all the emotions of what it means to see your baby cross the stage and receive their diploma are with you in this odd tension of celebration and mourning.

Yes, I said mourning—sometimes you need permission to mourn a happy thing. For eighteen years or more, you've been devoted to raising this child. Your love has been paid in blood and sweat and tears to arrive at this day. You've invested. You've been all in. Getting your child to graduation day didn't happen by accident. You have played a vital role in getting them where they are today. And now your role is shifting.

It's time to move on from one thing to a new thing, and it's okay to admit you're a little sad about moving on from something you loved (although, it's equally fine that some of you may be relieved). It's okay to cry. Your tears reveal something important so it's wise to pay attention. Pause to hear what they're telling you. Tears are a pressure valve, a release, a watery conversation about something that matters when plain old words won't do. That day in the grocery store facing a pyramid of Fuji apples, my tears were acknowledging my great love for my daughter, and that I would miss having her living under my roof.

Maybe you're facing an empty nest or maybe it will be a while before you're there, but you've caught a glimpse and you know it's coming. You're shaky about the unknowns, but I'll give you a word of counsel: being intentional and making plans for that season will serve you well.

Recently I was with a group of friends when talk shifted to our kids' graduation. I was inspired by our conversation to share a few thoughts I've learned along the way. So, while you're searching for the perfect graduation present to buy, consider a few more gifts they *need*. You can't buy these with dollars and cents but make no mistake: they do come at a cost.

1. Space. *Cut the ties that bind.* We live in a world where we can remain virtually tethered 24/7. But we were never designed to live with a permanent umbilical cord to our children. Do your children (and yourself) a huge favor by resisting the urge to stalk their social media accounts or call or text constantly when they go off to college or move out on their own. While checking in an appropriate amount is always fun, keep in mind that you've done your best to train them up in the way they should go, and now it's time to let them go.

2. Vision. *Imagine their future out loud.* For years you've been an unconscious student of your child, and you, better than anyone else, see their potential. You're well acquainted with their strengths and challenges. Because of your unique point of view, you can help your children imagine what fields of study or careers to pursue, especially if they're having difficulty imagining for themselves. Don't try to micromanage or control their choices, but if they're struggling with decisions about a major or vocation, tell them what you see. Point out their strong suits and how that might translate into a career. As you gently push them out of the nest, give them a bull's-eye.

3. Prayer. *Keep them near in your heart.* Praying for your young adult children is one of the best ways to keep them near in heart when they're no longer living at home.

Ecclesiastes 3 is one of my favorite passages of Scripture because it speaks to the ever-changing nature of life. One season spills into the next, sometimes in grand form and sometimes in quiet. Your child leaving home is a little of both: the ending of one thing, the beginning of another. A million tender moments and ever bittersweet.

A Love While Letting Them Fly

Hannah

> *On one occasion, Hannah got up after they ate and drank at Shiloh. The priest Eli was sitting on a chair by the doorpost of the LORD's temple. Deeply hurt, Hannah prayed to the LORD and wept with many tears. Making a vow, she pleaded, "LORD of Armies, if you will take notice of your servant's affliction, remember and not forget me, and give your servant a son, I will give him to the LORD all the days of his life, and his hair will never be cut."*
>
> 1 SAMUEL 1:9–11

Provoked and ridiculed, Hannah endured the shame that came with years of childlessness. She ran to the Lord, knowing He was the only One who could heal her pain and grant her heart's desire. When Hannah prayed to the Lord, she poured out her heart to God, and in her desperate desire for a son, Hannah vowed to give him back to the Lord. With deep compassion, the Lord heard her prayer and granted her request. After she weaned her son Samuel, she was faithful to bring him to the temple to be raised as a priest.

Hannah's faithfulness and bravery brought the priest who would anoint Israel's first two kings and shepherd the nation from the era of judges into the era of kings.

God knew what He was doing, even when the situation was painful and unclear. What a Master Planner! And what a brave, beautiful, and bold heart of love Hannah had for her son, and her God.

Reflections

How is God asking you to be brave through your circumstances?

_____

_____

_____

_____

_____

_____

_____

_____

_____

_____

_____

_____

_____

_____

_____

_____

_____

The Flip Side of Love

Whenever I read Hannah's story in the first chapter of 1 Samuel, followed by her triumphant prayer in the second chapter and subsequent stories about young Samuel, I am reduced to tears.

My husband and I tried for years to conceive. When it finally happened—we were pregnant!—it only lasted eleven weeks before dissolving in a traumatic and terrifying miscarriage. It took more than a year before we conceived again, and this time, our son was born at forty weeks exactly.

We named him Samuel, largely in part to this passage:

> *I prayed for this boy, and since the LORD gave me what I asked him for, I now give the boy to the LORD. For as long as he lives, he is given to the LORD.*

1 SAMUEL 1:27-28

I get Hannah. I get promising anything in desperate hope. And I get the pain that comes with following through—sort of. Hannah visited her Samuel once a year: ". . . each year his mother made him a little robe and took it to him when she went with her husband to offer the annual sacrifice" (1 Sam. 2:19). I see my son every day, but I'll never forget the bittersweet pang that came when he hopped on a school bus for the first time. I about bowled him over when he came home that afternoon; I can't imagine seeing him once a year. But Hannah joyfully (perhaps wistfully) let her Samuel fly. She praised the Lord, saying, "There is no one holy like the LORD. There is no one besides you! And there is no rock like our God" (v. 2).

It's not easy for me to let my children fly, and I wonder how easy it was for Hannah. God eventually gave her five more children, three sons and two daughters (v. 21). I wonder if Hannah found herself holding them a little closer, overwhelmed with thanks, and offering up praise that wasn't recorded in Scripture. I wonder if she actually became more reserved with her love, holding back in fear of the unthinkable. I wouldn't blame her if she did; I've been there, too.

My kids love the movie *Frozen*. They can narrate the film; I think I could recite it in my sleep. Every time we watch it and I hear Elsa say, "Conceal, don't feel, don't let it show," I think of how we use those words to stay safe. What do we lose and miss out on when we use such self-preservation? "Conceal, don't feel" froze Elsa with fear, isolated her, and left her icily alone and afraid. Those words stole her freedom.

They can do the same to us.

When I realize that I've been in a season of holding back love, I know I need to address some fears. It all comes from a self-preservation that's debilitating. I'm too happy. The shoe's going to drop. Any day now, something awful will happen. So don't get too happy, and don't love with all you've got. Just in case. That way it won't come as such a shock when the awful comes, and you won't be quite as hurt. Conceal, don't feel.

As a mother, wife, daughter, sister, friend—as one who loves anyone at all—we risk greatly when we love. We risk being offended and rejected and hurt. We risk pain and grief. We risk fumbling through disaster. But we take the risk, because the flip side of love is fear, and we follow in the steps of the One who took the greatest risk ever in loving us:

> *But God demonstrates his own love for us in this: While we were still sinners, Christ died for us.*
>
> ROMANS 5:8 (NIV)

Despite what God may receive from us, He chooses to love. Jesus concealed nothing and felt everything. Because of the way He has flipped the sides once and for all, we are also free to choose to be frozen or free.

Once in a while I whisper to my husband that our Samuel would've been enough. Our one little boy would've been enough to elicit from me the same measure of praise and thanks that Hannah prayed. God is a god of abundance, and He blessed us with two daughters as well.

One by one, my kids are growing their wings. They're making their own mistakes, paving their own way, owning their personalities and quirks, and I fall madly in love with them every day. Eventually I'll be able to identify even more deeply with Hannah, as my little birdies fly the coop and we enter a new season of life. But also, like Hannah, I'm hopeful that I will be able to burst with praise and pride at the heart my kids have for the Lord, and celebrate their good works and paths, and that I too may be able to give them back to the One from whom they came.

Reflections

How can you lean into joy instead of fear?

When Prayer Doesn't Seem Like Enough

For as long as I can remember, I've wanted to adopt. My dream has been to open our hearts and our home to a child who needs a forever family. I've started the process several times, too, but each time I sensed that my husband wasn't quite as enthusiastic about adoption as I was, so I felt it was wisest to wait (and pray) until we were both on board with the idea of adoption.

As the years went by, I kept asking God, "How long, Lord?"

Then one day it happened. My husband called me from work and told me about a friend who knew a friend who was pregnant. She was planning on giving up the baby for adoption, and she wanted to find a family. My husband wanted to know if it would be okay to tell his friend we were interested.

I could barely contain myself as my excitement burst through every word, "Yes! Of course!"

After all those years of waiting, and now my husband was the one initiating the process! I just knew this was from God. And, really, the timing couldn't have been better.

Lengthy conversations continued, and she said she wanted us to adopt her child, but there was another complication. A recent ultrasound showed there were two babies. She was having twins. Were we still interested?

Now I was crying, because I always wanted twins. "Yes! Double yes!" That was all I could say. That, and "Thank You, Lord!"

We contacted a social worker who could walk us through the paperwork, and the whole ball really got rolling. We continued to pray and dream, and some days, I found myself wandering down the baby aisle at Target, looking at two of everything.

The twins, we later learned, were girls. And I couldn't help it. Their names were already etched on my heart—Ella and Emma. So I started praying for Ella and Emma, and their birth mom, too.

And just when we started believing this was real, and this was really going to happen, it didn't. We knew failed adoptions happen, and we were warned to guard our hearts, you know, just in case. And honestly, I had tried to prepare myself for the possibility that it might not happen. But all the signs seemed to be pointing in the right direction. I really, truly believed this was a gift from God, and that He was completely in this.

But then it was all ripped away.

I've never had a miscarriage. I've never bled from a lost child. But when I realized Ella and Emma weren't coming home, that they weren't going to be a part of our family, my heart bled plenty.

For months (dare I say the next couple of years?) I felt an emptiness I couldn't describe. And I had lots of questions for God. Why would He put this desire in my heart only to take it all away? Why would He have me fall in love with two baby girls only to lose them in the end? None of it made sense.

I was a tangled mess of angry and sad, but mostly I was scared. Were they being cared for? Were they being fed? Were they being held? I was so worried for them, I could hardly think of anything else.

All I could do was pray. So I did. But I'll tell you, it didn't feel like enough.

I questioned the power of prayer because prayers are words. They may be sincere, heartfelt words. But babies don't need words from afar; they need warm bottles and clean diapers and soft blankets and lots of kisses.

Every time I prayed for God to protect them and provide for them, I felt so powerless, so frustrated that I couldn't make sure they were getting what they needed. And yet, during this time four faint words kept coming to mind, like whispers from somewhere deep in my soul.

Do you trust Me?

And therein lay the crux of my battle . . . I didn't want to release these two baby girls into God's care. I didn't want to trust anyone to take care of them except me.

For a long time afterward, I cried and grieved and wondered how they were doing. I'd pray too. Because that was literally the only thing I could do. But I still wanted to know why. Why did God let me fall in love with two baby girls only to take them away?

And then one day, in a quiet sort of way, I knew.

When I finally accepted that Ella and Emma weren't meant to be a part of our forever family, I understood they were meant to be a part of my forever heart. They don't know it, but they have someone, somewhere in the world, who is committed to praying for them, forever.

I don't know what their birth mom decided to name them, so Ella and Emma aren't even their real names, but I do know that when I pray for Ella and Emma, God knows exactly who I'm praying for.

And someday, on the other side of eternity, I pray I get to meet them.

Reflections

Lord, restore us to Yourself, so we may return; renew our days as in former times.

LAMENTATIONS 5:21 (HCSB)

What—or who—have you had to release to the Lord?

_____

_____

_____

_____

_____

_____

_____

_____

_____

_____

_____

_____

_____

_____

_____

_____

Lamentation

Years ago, I sat in the corner of a tiny break room off the hall of a hospital corridor. My husband, along with his two brothers and the hospital's representative sat together at one of those eight-foot long, all-purpose tables. I was there for moral support.

Down the hospital corridor, in a room right across from the nurse's station, my husband's mother lay in a bed, barely breathing. Her name was Nancy, but we called her Nano.

My husband and his brothers sat motionless at the table as Christina, the hospital's representative, shared with them what to expect in the hours ahead. As I sat in the corner, watching Christina (her name was not lost on me) gently describe what happens when our soul leaves our body for good, I watched the reality of her words sink into the hearts of the men around the table. Their shoulders slumped. Their jaws grew slack. They sat back in their seats, visibly blindsided even though it was hard to argue with what we'd seen as we stood at the bedside, holding Nano's hand, pressing our cheeks against hers, brushing back her silver hair, and whispering love notes into her ear.

When I leaned over the railing and pressed my cheek to hers, she pressed back, her soft skin warm against my own. But that was all there was. She had been sick before—hospitalized, even. In fact, there had been many times we thought, *This is it*. But she always rallied. So much so, I began to believe she'd outlive us all.

This time, as we stood by her bed, we all knew things were different.

In that break room Christina confirmed our suspicions and it took the wind out of our sails. I held in my sobs, but Christina, skilled in the work of leading loved ones into grief, caught my eyes and offered a sweet look of warm consolation as the tears coursed down my cheeks. By the time the men pulled themselves away from the table, I'd managed to wipe away the evidence of my grief. After all, I was there for moral support.

We gathered the family for their last good-byes and Nano was moved to a quiet room on the hospice floor. We sang and prayed, laughed and told stories. Then, as the hours marched on, with Nano still taking shallow breaths, the room slowly emptied until it was just my husband and Nano in that quiet hospital room.

My husband says the moment Nano's soul left her body, it was as if the room was filled with her presence and with a beautiful fragrance he could only call, Love.

Nano was the last of the generation before us. So we held our nieces and nephews and our own children as they returned to the hospice floor and sobbed at the news of Nano's passing. We rubbed their backs and squeezed their hands and looked deep into their eyes to remind them how much they'd been loved, and how well.

We held hands together in a circle around the bed to thank God for such a wonderful soul and such a powerful love.

Later, I held my husband as he cried and I listened to him tell the story, over and over again, of what a beautiful thing it had been—a privilege and an honor, he said—to have been with his mother when she died. And when the tears for the night were done, we slept.

In the morning, before I'd opened my eyes, my grief tore me open with deep sobs of lament. I'd held it in for far too long. My cries reached my own ears as something foreign and I struggled to catch my breath. My grief spilled from some place deep within me, and my husband

and daughter rushed to my side. I had awakened the household with my sorrow.

My grief ran rampant and someone pressed one tissue after another into my hand. That morning, I cried for hours, unable to speak without crumbling into sobs. No one shushed me. No one told me to pull myself together. Not even when I broke down in the restaurant later that morning. No one looked away from me. No one made me ashamed of my lament.

Lament is a gift we are given.

When the world gets heavy and our hearts break open, our chests heave with the weight, and we wail from the depths of the emptiness that remains. Our cries set us free and make space for the sweet, sweet ministry of the Spirit of God who is, Himself, love. And so, we are invited to mourn with those who mourn. Even when their method of lament is unfamiliar to us. When their lament makes us nervous or skeptical or sad or afraid, the words of Scripture invite us to pull up closer and join in, creating more and more space for the Spirit of God to come even closer with whispers of love.

I too had been loved so much and so well by Nano. The intensity of my sadness was a testimony to her mothering love. No wonder it was love that filled the room as she slipped from this world into the next. No wonder my lament was so deeply felt and so warmly welcomed by those who had loved her, too.

Reflections

Are you grieving? Have you been holding in your tears? Or, do you know someone who is mourning and would welcome your partnership in her grief?

_____

_____

_____

_____

_____

_____

_____

_____

_____

_____

_____

_____

_____

_____

V. *love*
around the Table

Is any place warmer to gather than around the table? Where bellies and hearts are both filled with nourishment and love? Where conversations are had and promises are met and the coffee is strong? The table is often seen as the heart of the home, a place where time is tracked by plates and cups, dishes full and emptied, forks clanking and chairs scraping, laughter ringing and voices mingling.

These stories bring us to our tables. They meet us in the kitchens of our past and the dining rooms of our present. They bring memories of loved ones gone Home and hopes of conversations yet to be had. Pull up a chair, pick up a mug, and see how God sits with us at the table.

Feasts with Grandma

My grandma was an excellent cook, and she welcomed me into the sanctuary of her kitchen. She taught me tricks for perfect mashed potatoes, how to make a Sunday roast, and that frozen lasagna is perfectly acceptable for company dinner. She set a beautiful table with her china, and she made a mean gravy from scratch. Holiday feasts at Grandma's included everything, from relish trays to rolls, a main course to several side dishes, and always a mouthwatering dessert.

Grandma never wrote down her recipes. She was very much a "pinch of this, dash of that" kind of cook. After she died, I came across a binder full of recipes she'd assembled from newspaper clippings, recipe cards from friends, and notes she'd jotted down at church potlucks. I even recognized a few dishes that she'd made with me at her side! I loved finding this treasure. Although she'd completely doctored up the actual recipes as she made them, the binder still brought me comfort and continues to do so from its spot on a shelf in my kitchen.

You see, it was never about the feasts she prepared. I mean, her food was amazing. But it was really about being with her. It was about spending time together, standing side by side at the stove. It was about my family gathered around her table, laughing and sharing stories. Going to Grandma's house for dinner was never really about the food; it was about being in the presence of goodness, peace, and joy.

That's what she really left behind for us to inherit. The memories of her goodness, her peace, and her joy are what endure. These are the legacies we will leave our kids, family, and friends.

So, write down those special recipes. Share your kitchen space with your kids. Invite family and friends to your table for the feasts of the season. And recognize the intangible gift and goodness that comes from being together, for this is the glory of the Kingdom.

TIPS FROM GRANDMA'S KITCHEN

- When making mashed potatoes, cut the potatoes into big chunks before boiling to cut down on cooking time.

- Don't shy away from shortcuts. They allowed Grandma to spend more time with those gathered around her table—frozen lasagnas, pre-chopped veggies, and bakery-fresh rolls were staples in her home. Feel free to use the same.

- Always leave a stick of butter in a covered dish on the counter. That way you're sure to have room temperature butter available when it's called for in a recipe.

- Welcome kids into the kitchen. The memories made will go far beyond the food.

For the Kingdom of God is not a matter

of what we eat or drink,

but of living a life of goodness and peace

and joy in the Holy Spirit.

ROMANS 14:17 (NLT)

Reflections

What intangible legacy do you hope to leave your family and friends?
What's one special recipe from your childhood that you could pass
along to the children in your life?

Becoming What We Behold

I go through dozens of Grandma's collected pieces of china, each one delicate and fine. And my mom has a story for each one:

"Oh, that was the candy dish! If I snuck a piece, I had to lift the silver lid just right, so it wouldn't make any noise."

"She set out that dish and filled it with nuts, served with this silver spoon at every church ladies' circle meeting."

"She put mashed potatoes in that bowl!"

I scour the Internet for details on the precious china and glassware, and what I find makes me gasp. Each piece is worth actual dollars! Some pieces are worth several actual dollars! The day I loaded her white Haviland china into the back of the minivan, I drove almost as carefully as the day we brought our firstborn from the hospital.

As I set each dish, plate, and cup in its new home in my china hutch, I pause to really look at them—and marvel at what I see. Light and tiny but very much present atop of plates are lines where knives scraped across them decades ago. *She actually used these!* I think.

And that thought strikes me hard, because I am a saver.

Gardenia perfume I wore on my wedding day? I spritz it on my wrists only on our anniversary. Beautiful teacup from my wedding shower? I haven't used it since. Crisp white linen napkins, received for our engagement? I only bring them out for Christmas dinner. All these gifts, literally collecting dust.

Most likely, their giver wouldn't be too happy if they knew their gifts were just taking up space instead of bringing joy on a regular basis.

While some things are more meaningful when held onto, the idea of leaving my best things unused doesn't sit well in my heart. Because if I can't bring myself to use the good dishes on a Tuesday night, what else do I hoard and squirrel away? My best listening ear, reserved for only dear friends in crisis. The best of my servant's heart, reserved for those who can somehow serve me back. The best of my God-given gifts, reserved to the point where they become buried, and I argue when He asks me to use them.

It's as though we believe the things we save could save us.

> *"Don't hoard treasure down here where it gets eaten by moths and corroded by rust or—worse!—stolen by burglars. Stockpile treasure in heaven, where it's safe from moth and rust and burglars. It's obvious, isn't it? The place where your treasure is, is the place you will most want to be, and end up being."*
>
> MATTHEW 6:19-21 (MSG)

I've heard it said that "You become what you behold"—wisdom from 2 Corinthians 3:18. What am I becoming if I am holding back the best of my things, and the best of myself—both out of fear?

My grandma never held back. She brought out the good plates and lit the candles on the dining room table for lasagna dinner on Wednesday nights. She always had a full candy dish waiting for us. She never withheld her listening ear or her love. Her warm and wrinkled hands were ready for holding, and her arms open wide for hugs. She was generous with her love, her time, and her costume jewelry collection.

There is deep power in the loving of others, and we are able to both give and receive that when we gather around the table and give our best.

Grandma's dishes now live in my china hutch and kitchen cupboards. Over time, I will add to the faint knife scrapes on the plates, so that when my kids go through them in sixty years, they too will have stories to tell.

Reflections

What are you holding on to, saving for a special day? How can you use those things instead of allowing them to collect dust?

Love around the Table

The Widow of Zarephath

"Get up, go to Zarephath that belongs to Sidon and stay there. Look, I have commanded a woman who is a widow to provide for you there." So Elijah got up and went to Zarephath. When he arrived at the city gate, there was a widow gathering wood. Elijah called to her and said, "Please bring me a little water in a cup and let me drink." As she went to get it, he called to her and said, "Please bring me a piece of bread in your hand."

But she said, "As the Lord your God lives, I don't have anything baked—only a handful of flour in the jar and a bit of oil in the jug. Just now, I am gathering a couple of sticks in order to go prepare it for myself and my son so we can eat it and die."

Then Elijah said to her, "Don't be afraid; go and do as you have said. But first make me a small loaf from it and bring it out to me. Afterward, you may make some for yourself and your son, for this is what the Lord God of Israel says, 'The flour jar will not become empty and the oil jug will not run dry until the day the Lord sends rain on the surface of the land.'"

So she proceeded to do according to the word of Elijah. Then the woman, Elijah, and her household ate for many days. The flour jar did not become empty, and the oil jug did not run dry, according to the word of the LORD he had spoken through Elijah.

1 KINGS 17:9–16

The woman Elijah met at the gate of Sidon had nothing to give. She and her son were starving, and she had nothing to offer him, let alone anyone else. So when Elijah asked her for water and bread, she turned him down. What else could she do? But when Elijah insisted, promising there would be enough, she shared with him what little she had.

Hospitality, for her, meant sacrifice. But God is always faithful to provide for His people when He asks them to share with others. God provided for the woman, her son, and Elijah with a jug of oil and a jar of flour that did not run dry until the drought ended. Because of her hospitality and God's faithfulness, they had everything they needed.

This widow knew how to welcome both strangers and family to her table, and as this Scripture passage shows, all benefited from her welcome.

Reflections

When have you trusted God to provide? Have you ever sacrificed in the name of welcoming others to your table?

_____

_____

_____

_____

_____

_____

_____

_____

_____

_____

_____

_____

_____

_____

_____

_____

Breaking the Mold of Perfection

As moms, we are writing the stories of others. When I realized that I was the one responsible for creating the memories my kids would someday look back on with nostalgia, I panicked. I've settled down since the second and third kids arrived (it's a necessity), but for a while I was all aboard the perfection train, trying to make my life and memories line up with the picture-perfect feeds we see all over social media.

With a history of unexplained infertility and miscarriages, my husband and I weren't sure if we'd be able to have more kids, so when our son turned one, I threw the bash of the year. I worked for weeks to get ready, invited more than fifty people, and worked myself into a Pinterest-induced frenzy to make everything perfect. I decorated. I created custom invitations. I planned the food and cooked and shopped 'til I dropped.

I actually placed itty-bitty, teeny-weeny blue sugar snowflakes on three dozen white chocolate covered cookies, attaching each snowflake with a tiny drop of pearly white frosting.

And the morning of his party, I woke up with strep throat.

The party was perfect and beautiful, but I hardly remember it because of my illness haze. I was trying to write a story of perfection instead of focusing on celebrating our son with sweet family and friends.

Since that December we've had countless more birthday parties, and I'm proud to say that we've bought the cakes, barely decorated the house, and I haven't been sick at a single party. I've stuck with focusing on the celebrating, and doing only the extra things that actually bring me joy.

I realized my kids wouldn't remember the details of perfect birthday parties, but they would remember if their mom was a train wreck.

Recently we had friends over to stay with us. We live near the airport, and they had a morning flight, so it was a great excuse for a sleepover. We held each other's babies, we sat in the kitchen and talked until midnight, and we shared crackers right out of the bag. Their room had clean sheets and an avalanche behind the closet door. Dirty dishes were piled in the sink and overflowing right out of it onto the counter, all the way to the stove top. We had vacuumed up the dog hair, but left coats slung over the banisters and a package delivered earlier that day smack dab in the middle of the kitchen floor. *I wasn't even home when they arrived!*

It was absolutely not the definition of perfect, but it was just right. My family was in the middle of a very busy, burning-the-midnight oil kind of week, and our friends stepped right into the thick of it. Because that's exactly where true friends belong.

The thing is, I didn't bat an eyelash and neither did they. We hugged, big belly-to-belly hugs, and laughed and dove into deep conversation, right there in our real. The mess didn't matter because in that moment, actually being with our friends mattered more.

This was my first hint that something was softening inside my heart. That something, the thing that would drive me to run myself ragged cleaning before company came—that thing was slowly dissolving.

And my kids had front-row seats.

At a conference I attended several years ago, one of the keynote speakers was addressing true hospitality when she said something that literally took my breath away. "True hospitality," she said, "is when your guests leave your home feeling better about themselves, not feeling better about you."

Those words left her mouth and punched me right in the stomach.

So often—nearly every time I entertain—I am a hot mess before the guests arrive. I whirl around the house, scrubbing and cleaning and arranging. I plan my meal and make a time chart so things are ready upon their arrival. I snap at my husband and plunk the kids in front of the TV so they're not in my way. I don't welcome my kids into the kitchen with me, as I can do it faster and right the first time. Ugh. Do I want to create a lovely, warm, and welcoming atmosphere for my guests? Of course. Do I want them to leave feeling better about me? I do.

But no more.

Sometimes letting go of expectations, especially around a table, can be hard for me. I want the table to be lovely, the meal to be impressive, and basically everything pretty close to perfect. At times I've sacrificed the happiness of my family to chase that perfection. I've stretched myself far too thin in the name of making memories and writing perfectly ideal stories. But that's not what I want my kids to remember.

I want my kids to see me giving thanks, to see me making room for friends and family in our home, right there amidst the to-do list and the dust bunnies.

I'm over trying to fit into a perfect mold of what I thought gatherings are supposed to look like, because there is no mold.

As a memory maker, my job isn't to chase or create perfection. It's to find the beauty in our real-life days and make sure my kids experience it, too.

That's where their stories will come from.

Reflections

What areas of perfection are you willing to drop? What do you think you'll actually gain if those areas are less than perfect?

_____

_____

_____

_____

_____

_____

_____

_____

_____

_____

_____

_____

_____

_____

_____

_____

The Least of These

What would I do if someone knocked on my door and told me they were hungry? I like to think my response would be eager and immediate. I would whip up sandwiches. I would fill a paper sack with bananas and peanut butter and cheese sticks. I would even throw in a box of my children's favorite cereal.

I can remember sometimes doing almost exactly that when we lived in an apartment near the center of a large city. In those days, we had a friend from church who occasionally dropped by to chat or to read us his latest poem. On a few occasions, he rang our buzzer because his family had stumbled into the gap between their grocery budget and his next paycheck. On those visits, I always made him a sandwich, and I always packed a bag with food for his three girls. Thanks to his friendship, I have good reason to believe I would do the right thing for a hungry stranger today.

In the parable where the sheep and the goats get sorted out, Jesus sets a test for "the nations":

> *"And the King will answer them, 'Truly I tell you, whatever you did for one of the least of these brothers and sisters of mine, you did for me.'"*
> MATTHEW 25:40

Some scholars suggest that "the least of these" in this context might refer only to suffering believers, "these brothers and sisters of mine," while other experts see a more universal brotherhood of the needy. As I've studied these debates, it has been helpful for me to remember the surprise of the people being sorted. Their astonishment suggests that Christ will appear to us when and where we least expect it.

Compassion comes naturally to me, and I have always assumed that compassion was a spiritual test I could ace. After all, when a church friend needed help in between paychecks, I didn't close my hand to him. Yet when a different sort of test came, I almost failed. I had forgotten to look for Christ where I least expected to find Him. And who, after all, would say no to a hungry child? Who would say no to their own hungry child? Me, apparently. When my ten-year-old son turned his deep brown eyes in my direction and said he wanted pumpkin pie on Thanksgiving dinner, I told him no.

My son is often hungry, though not because our pantry isn't full. He hungers for all the foods he is allergic to: pizza topped with gooey cheese, peanut butter sandwiches, pecan pie like his grandmother bakes, frosted birthday cake, and, as I discovered, pumpkin pie. I was already overwhelmed by turkey-brining and gravy-making.

When our Thanksgiving guests offered to bring the pies, I gratefully accepted. I knew my son would not be able to eat those floury crusts and creamy fillings, so I had picked up a box of allergen-free cookies. When he saw that box sitting on the shelf, he whispered, "But Mom, I've never tasted pumpkin pie."

I held firm for two days. I did not have time to go back to the grocery store. He probably wouldn't even like pumpkin pie. It would require researching gluten-free, dairy-free pie recipes. Why go to all that trouble, when I had so many other dishes to make?

My son didn't whine, and he didn't beg. Perhaps that's why I finally gave in. Yet even after I had found a recipe, even after I had driven to the grocery store, my testing wasn't finished. Because my chatty, four-year-old daughter wanted, desperately, to help me bake that pie, I became frazzled and distracted. It was only after I placed the whole cinnamon-scented thing in the preheated oven that I noticed the unopened bag of sugar sitting on my kitchen counter. Pumpkin may be the most important ingredient in pumpkin pie, but surely sugar is a close second.

I had tried. Wasn't that good enough? Clearly, I wasn't required to go back to the grocery store. Certainly, I wasn't required to make *yet another pie.* There must be a verse in the Bible somewhere that says, "Thanks. You did your best. No need to feel guilty that you couldn't do more," right?

I stood at the kitchen counter staring at that bag of sugar for quite a while. I was sure I did not owe my son a pumpkin pie. The most likely scenario was that he would take one bite and declare that he did not like pumpkin pie after all. And then he would ask for cookies.

I might not have earned an A+ on this spiritual test, but I was sure I'd managed at least a passing grade. As I dumped the pie into the trash bin, the questions I asked suddenly shifted in my mind. Instead of "how much do I owe my son?" I found myself asking, "how much do I love my son?" I had not considered the most important part of Jesus' parable. I wasn't baking that pie for just anyone. I was baking it for Jesus Himself as He reached out to me in the form of my own freckle-nosed child. This wasn't a test. This was an opportunity.

I baked another pie, and my son pronounced it delicious. Though, I acknowledge, it was my husband who sweetly offered to make that second trip to the grocery store. Love is rarely lonely work. There is fellowship in suffering, there is fellowship in serving, and Jesus might already be so much nearer than we thought, in a face and in a request we'd never expect.

Better with Peace

"Why do we even waste our money?" my husband asked me after once again reprimanding our four children at the nice restaurant we had taken them to for a special treat.

They were not grateful. They were fighting over who got to write on the paper that covered the white linen tablecloth, and they were whining about having to split a meal or wanting to change seats or even go home. It seemed every time we tried to take them to an expensive restaurant, they were worse. As much as I love the experience of restaurants—especially the part where I don't have to clean up—the truth was, I was miserable.

As much as I tried to make magical, Instagrammable memories around a certain special event, I found that most of our best memories as a family happened when we had simple fun. It might be laughing over a funny comment during dessert or a perfectly timed hug while cleaning the dishes after dinner. Maybe that is what the writer means when he says, "Better a dry crust with peace than a house full of feasting with strife" (Prov. 17:1 CSB). It is not simply the food that makes a great meal, just as it is not merely the outward adornments of a house that make a home.

At the heart of peace is harmony. To be at peace with someone—whether a friend, a coworker, a family member, or God—is to be in a harmonious relationship with them. When we ask God to cleanse us of our sin and make us new creations, we are asking for a harmonious relationship with Jesus, the ultimate peace giver, because He is peace.

I want our table and home to be a place where people feel free to be themselves and where they know that, although it may not always be quiet, it is full of contentment and peace. We are grateful for what God has given us and who God created us to be to glorify Him. Our table, more than perfect napkins, is better when it is set with peace.

Our kids are older now. They do not fight over the crayons, and they can each eat a whole meal by themselves. Our conversations have changed from who is sitting where to the things going on in their lives. Whether we are at home eating with our kids and the friends they invited home from college, or eating a great feast where the food is made in front of you, we are living in the moment with each other. We are grateful to the One who welcomes us to His table of feasting and of doing life with Him. That kind of peace makes any meal special!

Memories around the Table

When my grandpa was dying, the first in his family to reach age ninety, my family gathered at the hospital. We didn't leave his side for hours, and didn't leave the hospital for days. Back then there were no little kids yet, only my mom and siblings and spouses. A family of adult children gathered to mourn and celebrate our dear grandpa as he made his way Home. The day before my grandpa slipped away to reunite with his Lord and his beloved wife and siblings, my husband left the hospital to fetch food. We were drained, and sad, and tired of vending machine sustenance.

Of all places, he went to McDonald's and returned with a feast like we'd never experienced. We piled the food on a tiny table in the hospital waiting room, and as we ate, we also laughed. We stopped crying. We felt like kids in a candy shop, devouring cheeseburgers and fries with gusto and joy. Gathered around a table, our hearts were as full as our stomachs.

***

Growing up, on every first day of school, Easter, birthday, and Christmas morning, my mom would pull a tube of refrigerated cinnamon rolls from the fridge and bake them, filling the house with the scent of sweet cinnamon and dough. The icing dripped onto our plates, those rolls an immediate indicator of a special day ahead.

The smell of cinnamon rolls still (and instantly) brings me back to those days, when the biggest fight my siblings and I would have was over who would get the roll from the middle of the pan. I've still not mastered (or even tried, to be honest) making cinnamon rolls from scratch, because good enough is good enough. I love the idea of my kids associating being warm and cozy with both special days and with regular snowy Tuesday mornings. Gathered around a table, the warmth from fresh-from-the-oven rolls fills our tummies as joy fills our souls.

***

My grandma had four sisters. The five Johnson girls were close for their whole lives, until death began to separate them. My siblings and I were blessed to have a front-row seat to their friendship, attending gatherings that always began around a table. Those five sisters knew how to truly host family—the dining room table holding a meal that was going to be memorable. Well, one of the sisters was not quite the cook that the others were, so we knew when we went to her house to eat a peanut butter and jelly sandwich on the way, and another on the way home! But no matter the food, it was the company that really filled everyone.

At one such gathering, my sister (about five years old at the time) coined the group of five sisters "the laughing ladies." That nickname stuck for the rest of their years, and today she and I make up our own version of the laughing ladies. My kids know that when I sit at a table with my mom and sister, we won't move for hours except to refill the mugs or grab tissues to wipe tears (from sharing tender stories and moments), and that our laughter will ring from us gathered around the table.

***

Hundreds of holidays—turkey at Thanksgiving, ham on Easter, appetizers on Christmas Eve, prime rib on Christmas Day. Cakes, both store-bought and homemade, on birthdays. Thousands of cups of coffee, some spilled, some left to cool as conversation went deep, others refilled and lingered over into the night. Book clubs that never made it to the living room couches, staying instead around the food and the table that held it. Homework struggled over, tears shed, laughter loud. Joyful celebrations and quiet reflections. Countless moments in between. These things are what tables are made of.

What memories have you made around your table? What memories are your kids making around your table?

Reflections

How do you hope people feel when they're gathered around your table?

Kitchen Therapy

Baking is therapy for my soul. My husband knows that after a long day, he may find me in the kitchen whipping up a pecan pie, chocolate chip cookies, cranberry-apple crisp, or raspberry jam bars.

Baking is kind of magical. Taking the tasteless—*flour, eggs, baking powder or soda*—and adding that which doesn't taste good by itself—*salt, oil, vinegar*. Dropping in intense flavors that call for other ingredients to tone them down—*sugar, vanilla, cinnamon, zested citrus*—and seeing that the finished product needed all the ingredients, that together they are better than they were on their own.

Apron tied around my waist, which is softer than ever. The kitchen swelling with scents, messes, laughter, heat, love. My kids running in and out, scooting around the floor, playing with plastic cups and refrigerator magnets, reading cookbooks, and desperate to help add a pinch, mix, stir, dust surfaces with flour, and use old woven potholders as we bake up recipes from my grandma.

Baking together muddles time. The techniques are the same as hers—my grandma with the softest hands and dinner rolls. Though she's been gone for a decade, her life continues to intersect with mine here in my kitchen as we bake the same recipes that her mom's mom made, probably as her own babies crawled on the floor. I wonder how many times she had to experiment before she knew just how much flour and butter to add in order to make impossibly crumbly shortbreads and rich crusts.

On their own, butter is just yellow fat, and flour is just ground wheat. But once stirred with my mixer, butter and flour become cookies, cream-colored and sitting sweetly on a plate.

We too, this family, are better together than we are on our own.

I soften. He slows. Together is our favorite way to be; it's where I am the best version of myself because it's the real one. Our worst parts burn bright, yes, but together, our goods are better and our better, really good. There's no start to him and end to me—we're just one us. Batter in the oven, we dance in the spice-laced kitchen. We gaze at the grinning kids seated expectantly at the table, old dog at our feet, all looking at us joy-filled. Those kids are the best parts of us both.

In baking, we create new things—good things—and isn't that what God does in and through each of us? Isn't that exactly what God is up to in our kitchen, at our tables, and really, in our hearts?

Space at the Table

I stood, eight years old, at my mom's elbow as she stirred spaghetti sauce. It bubbled and sputtered all over the stove as she tasted, seasoned, and tasted again. She taught me both how to stretch a recipe, and how to laugh off the burned-black cookies. Weeknight dinner or Sunday lunch—our family was always together, passing our plates and teasing each other between bites. It was loud and beautiful.

Beyond stirring, mixing, and chopping at the family table, I learned there is always enough room.

Our table's heavy wooden leaf sat comfortably in the corner of the room, ready to make space. Space for more of us and our friends who were always welcome. Not one time do I recall my mother saying there wasn't enough to share.

One of my tall, tan brothers would often cruise through the kitchen, clink the lid of the cookie jar and mention that guy-from-school's parents were out of town and could he join us? Sure, she'd say, as she reached in the cabinet for one more can of tomatoes. The answer was always yes. The sauce was stirred, the leaf added to the table, and another plate pulled from the cabinet. I grew up having my arm graze the one next to me. Elbow room was a non-issue compared to reaching out and making space for others.

Now I'm the mom stirring the sauce, and I think of that table often.

What if we continued to make space at the table?

May we never mind rubbing elbows and sharing ourselves with one another. We are the body of Christ—made up of all our different, broken, and mended parts. Not only do we need each other, we are made far better by being together.

And when we make space for one another, we may just find a lot more room for God Himself to be in our midst.

How are you making space at your table?

Author Bios

Amanda White, ohamanda.com. Contributor to the *(in)courage Devotional Bible*. Wife. Mama. Bookworm and homeschooler resting in the shadow of the Almighty.

"A Beautiful Friendship," adapted from an article in the *(in)courage CSB Devotional Bible* (Nashville: Holman Bible Publishers, 2018), 1404.

Angie Ryg, angieryg.com. Contributor to the *(in)courage Devotional Bible*. Wife. Mom of four. Lover of her family, God's Word, and caramel lattes.

"Better with Peace," adapted from an article in the (in)courage CSB Devotional Bible (Nashville: Holman Bible Publishers, 2018), 879.

Anna Rendell, annarendell.com. (in)courage Contributor and Contributor to the *(in)courage Devotional Bible*. Author. Speaker. Digital Content Manager at (in)courage. Mom of three, running on grace and caffeine.

"Mothering Is . . . ," originally published on incourage.me at https://www.incourage.me/2018/09/mothering-is.html.

"Tiny Acts of Service, Big Celebration," adapted from the original publication on incourage.me at https://www.incourage.me/2018/05/hear-us-roar.html.

"First a Friend, Then a Family"

"Grit and Grace," adapted from the original publication on incourage. me at https://www.incourage.me/2016/02/on-lessons-from-twelve-weeks-with-three.html.

"Why I Don't Treasure Every Moment," adapted from the original publication on annarendell.com at http://annarendell.com/2015/06/will-treasure-kids-maybe-moments/.

"An Invitation to Be Beautiful," adapted from the original publication on incourage.me at https://www.incourage.me/2018/02/invitation-beautiful-archived.html.

"There's Nothing Balanced about Grace," adapted from the original publication on annarendell.com at https://annarendell.com/2017/05/no-thing-balance-whole-lot-grace/.

"The Worst Kind of Mommy War," originally published on annarendell.com at http://annarendell.com/2015/04/on-the-worst-kind-of-mommy-war/.

"#RealMomConfessions"

"The Holiness of Slow," originally published on incourage.me at https://www.incourage.me/2019/03/the-holiness-of-slow.html.

"Rest Is Best," adapted from an article in *One-Minute Devotions for Mothers: 365 Daily Moments with God* (Siloam Springs: DaySpring, 2019), 121.

"Take Real Care of Your Real Self"

"Trust God with All Your Heart," adapted from an article in the *(in)courage CSB Devotional Bible* (Nashville: Holman Bible Publishers, 2018), 853.

"Back-to-School," adapted from an article in *Pumpkin Spice for Your Soul: 25 Devotions for Autumn* (Minneapolis: Anna Rendell, 2018), 9.

"The Flip Side of Love," originally published on incourage.me at https://www.incourage.me/2014/06/on-the-flip-side-of-love.html.

"Feasts with Grandma," adapted from an article in *Pumpkin Spice for Your Soul: 25 Devotions for Autumn* (Minneapolis: Anna Rendell, 2018), 77.

"Tips from Grandma's Kitchen," adapted from an article in *Pumpkin Spice for Your Soul: 25 Devotions for Autumn* (Minneapolis: Anna Rendell, 2018), 79.

"Becoming What We Behold"

"Breaking the Mold of Perfection," adapted from an article in *A Moment to Breathe: 365 Devotions That Meet You in Your Everyday Mess* (Nashville: B&H Publishing Group, 2017) 23.

"Memories around the Table"

"Kitchen Therapy"

Christie Purifoy, christiepurifoy.com. Contributor to the *(in)courage Devotional Bible*. Wife. Mother. Author of *Roots and Sky: A Journey Home in Four Seasons*. Podcaster. Gardener.

"The Least of These," adapted from an article in the *(in)courage CSB Devotional Bible* (Nashville: Holman Bible Publishers, 2018), 1354.

Cynthia Stuckey, happygostuckey.com. (in)courage guest author. Writer. Reader. Blue House Dweller.

"Space at the Table," originally published on incourage.me at https://www.incourage.me/2015/08/a-table-with-leaves.html.

Dawn Camp, dawncamp.com. (in)courage contributor. Camera-toting mother of eight. Lover of gummy bears, sweet tea, good books, and movie dates.

"To Train Up a Child," originally published on incourage.me at https://www.incourage.me/2019/02/to-train-up-a-child.html.

Deidra Riggs, deidrariggs.com. (in)courage alum. Author. Speaker. Disco-lover.

"Lamentation," originally published on incourage.me at https://www.incourage.me/2017/02/sunday-scripture-69.html.

Denise J. Hughes, denisejhughes.com. (in)courage alum. Editor of and contributor to the *(in)courage Devotional Bible*. Author of *Deeper Waters* and the Bible study series Word Writers. Writer for the First 5 app by Proverbs 31 Ministries. Fan of peach tea, old books, and a good football game.

"When Prayer Doesn't Seem Like Enough," originally published on incourage.me at https://www.incourage.me/2017/11/when-prayer-doesnt-feel-life-enough.html.

"A Love That Breaks the Mold: Jochebed and Pharaoh's Daughter," adapted from an article in the *(in)courage CSB Devotional Bible* (Nashville: Holman Bible Publishers, 2018), 88.

"A Love That Breaks the Mold: Ruth and Naomi," adapted from an article in the *(in)courage CSB Devotional Bible* (Nashville: Holman Bible Publishers, 2018), 359, 363.

"A Love While Holding Them Close: Mary and Elizabeth," adapted from an article in the *(in)courage CSB Devotional Bible* (Nashville: Holman Bible Publishers, 2018), 1409, 1433.

"A Love While Letting Them Fly: Hannah," adapted from an article in the *(in)courage CSB Devotional Bible* (Nashville: Holman Bible Publishers, 2018), 369.

"A Love around the Table," adapted from an article in the *(in)courage CSB Devotional Bible* (Nashville: Holman Bible Publishers, 2018), 488.

Elisa Pulliam, moretobe.com. Contributor to the *(in)courage Devotional Bible*. Advocating for lives and legacies changed by God. Wife. Mom. Life coach. Mentor. Author. Speaker.

"Choosing to Thrive", adapted from an article in the *(in)courage CSB Devotional Bible* (Nashville: Holman Bible Publishers, 2018), 1592.

Jasmine Martin, instagram.com/jasminemartin. Contributor to the *(in)courage Devotional Bible*. Wife. Mom of five. Grace enthusiast. Photographer. Lover of words and iced coffee.

"A Different Kind of Brave," adapted from an article in the *(in)courage CSB Devotional Bible* (Nashville: Holman Bible Publishers, 2018), 90.

Karina Allen, forhisnameandhisrenown.wordpress.com. (in)courage contributor. Devoted to helping women live out their unique calling and building community through practical application of Scripture.

"For Motherless Daughters," originally published on incourage.me at https://www.incourage.me/2014/05/for-motherless-daughters.html.

Liz Curtis Higgs, lizcurtishiggs.com. (in)courage alum. *(in)courage Devotional Bible* contributor. Former bad girl, grateful for God's grace. Bible teacher, grateful for God's truth.

"When Nothing is Left but Love," adapted from an article in the *(in)courage CSB Devotional Bible* (Nashville: Holman Bible Publishers, 2018), 360.

Melissa Michaels, theinspiredroom.net. (in)courage alum. Author of *Love the Home You Have, Simple Gatherings,* and the award-winning blog *The Inspired Room.*

"Eighteen Summers," originally published on incourage.me at https://www.incourage.me/2017/06/eighteen-summers-2.html.

Robin Dance, robindance.me. (in)courage contributor. Wife, mama, and curious believer. She cares deep, loves wide, laughs often, and makes a wicked apple pie.

"When It's Time to Send," originally published on incourage.me at https://www.incourage.me/2018/04/when-its-time-to-send.html.

Sally Clarkson, sallyclarkson.com. Contributor to the *(in)courage Devotional Bible*. Mom of four. Wife of Clay. Author. Blogger. Podcaster (*At Home with Sally*). Mentoring women to know God's love.

"The Secret to Reaching Hearts," adapted from an article in the *(in)courage CSB Devotional Bible* (Nashville: Holman Bible Publishers, 2018), 1506.

Wynter Pitts, forgirlslikeyou.com. Contributor to the *(in)courage Devotional Bible*. Wife. Mom of four girls. Author of *She Is Yours*. Founder of *For Girls Like You* magazine and resources for girls.

"Surrender and Seek" adapted from an article in the *(in)courage CSB Devotional Bible* (Nashville: Holman Bible Publishers, 2018), 1314.

(in)courage welcomes you

to a place where authentic, brave women
connect deeply with God and others.
Through the power of shared stories and
meaningful resources, (in)courage champions
women and celebrates the strength Jesus gives
to live out our calling as God's daughters.
In the middle of your unfine moments and ordinary days,
you are invited to become a woman of courage.

Join us at **www.incourage.me** and
connect with us on social media!

@incourage

The CSB (in)courage Devotional Bible invites every woman to find her story *within the* greatest story ever told—God's story *of* redemption.

- **312 devotions** by 122 (in)courage community writers

- 10 distinct thematic **reading plans**

- Stories of courage from **50 women** of the Bible

- *and more features!*

Find out more at **incourageBible.com**

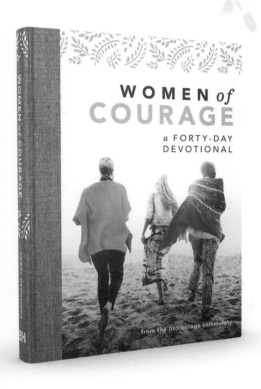

You are a Woman *of* Courage...
Because God says so.

Featuring 40 brave women from the Bible, this devotional will walk with you through the hardest days and leave you with the courage you need to lead, to love, to trust, and to turn to God in every situation.

Available now wherever books are sold.